The Unfulfilled Dream

Contents

Acknowledgements

My personal thanks to the following

IAN R. CARR
for putting all this together

PHIL NEILL
Is there a better artist?

'UNITED REVIEW'

TO MY FAMILY
Barbara, Duncan, Martin, Claire, Sam,
Evie, Aila, Harvey, Jean, Jayne and Lauren.

In Memory of
TONY ELLIS

Introduction

Fifty six years on the memory of Matt Busby's Babes team which dominated English football for a far too short period for Manchester United, still lives on.

Busby had joined a club without even a ground at the end of the Second World War, just over ten years later he had produced a team which lifted two League titles, were controversially deprived of a 'double' and reached the European Cup Semi Final. This followed on to his first side produced after the war which had won the FA Cup in 1948 and a League title in 1952. Behind all this, he had a reserve side that could have competed in the Football League and won the FA Youth Cup every season for its five years existence.

A young, vibrant, attractive side was about to become the envy of the whole football world until a catastrophic disaster at the end of Munich Airport on 6th February 1958 ended an unfulfilled dream.

The story of how these players had evolved from youngsters leaving school to being as the top players in the land is here for all to read in a diary of their two championship seasons. There is also the thought of what might have been as the likes of Denis Law, Bobby Charlton and George Best could have joined Duncan Edwards.

Roy James Cavanagh MBE
Worsley, June 2014

Chapter ONE

Champions

Old Trafford, Manchester, Saturday 7th April 1956

A pivotal meeting at the top of the Division One between Manchester United and Blackpool was about to take place without the man who had made this Manchester United side, their manager Matt Busby. He had to go back to Glasgow for a family bereavement, leaving his trusty lieutenant Jimmy Murphy to look after matters, a situation he was, sadly, have to do even more twenty two months on...

The position at the top of the league saw Manchester United in a fairly comfortable position as the two sides went into the last three matches of the season, four in Blackpool's case as they had a game in hand. At kick off, United had 55 points from 39 matches, with Blackpool on 49 points after 38 matches, two points for a win in those days; a victory for The Seasiders though would make the last couple of matches a bit twitchy.

Around lunch time, my Uncle Tom Perry called round to our two up, two down house off Ordsall Lane near to the Trafford Bridge, asking did I fancy going to the match.

Did I want to go? Too right I did, as a lad close to his ninth birthday the chance to go again to Old Trafford to see this emerging side, already tagged the 'Busby Babes' was something already a big part of my life. As we went down Ordsall Lane, all the green buses were lining up having brought the fans to the match, now waiting to take them back to various areas of Salford or into the city of Manchester. When you got to Trafford Bridge, which took you into the sprawling Trafford Park, a complex of warehouses and engineering factories which made the area a pivotal industrial zone, with railway lines moving commodities through, programme sellers were distributing the 'United Review'. A copy was already a must for me and we moved on towards the stadium. The morning rain had dried up and the scene was set for a memorable afternoon.

All ticket matches were not the norm in those days, and it was pay at the gate for the majority, with only the main stand alongside one of those railway lines being seated. Those gates were opened two hours before the game and massive crowds were already building up. We walked around the ground before finding a chance to get in at the Stretford End, which then was a sprawling open ended part of the ground. When you got inside you climbed loads of stairs before reaching the top to look down on the famous Old Trafford pitch. Well, that was the idea, but when we got there a sheer wall of supporters was in front of us. There was no way a little nine year old could get anywhere near the front, or indeed see much of the match! The gates were closed fifteen minutes before the start with 62,277 inside and an estimated 10,000 locked out with police struggling to maintain control outside the stadium.

So, Matt Busby and I both had to have a commentary of the match, Matt from a telephone link with reporter Arthur Walmsley, and myself from the noise in front of me and information given by my uncle. The first thing I was told was that the Blackpool mascot was a live duck that had a minder dressed as an Eastern Prince! Behind the Stretford End in those days was the Glovers Cables factory so I turned to watch their work side play on the day the top two sides in England played out a game for the league title!

Over the years I have picked lots of information from what actually happened, no Match of the Day, Talk Sport, mobiles in those times remember. I have the 'Football Pink' from after the match, printed within minutes of the end of the game, although this one must have been an issue on standby as it had tributes on some of its pages to the United side hailing them on becoming 'Champions'. Manchester United had prepared for the game as they normally did for major games by having a couple of days at the home of that days' visitors, Blackpool. Busby's side was unchanged, Blackpool having to make a change at right back where promising Jimmy Armfield, a Manchester lad and later an England captain, was ruled unfit and was replaced by David Frith. United's right back was a young man from the Oldham area who had broken the mould of Matt Busby's regular defence when he had replaced Billy Foulkes earlier in the season. His name? Ian Greaves. In later times I met Ian when he was the very successful manager of Bolton Wanderers. He told me of his memories of this title match.

"To think I played in some marvellous games as a team mate of such wonderful players like Roger Byrne, Bobby Charlton and the greatest of them all, Duncan Edwards, thrilled me" Ian had been brought into the side for the last fourteen matches of the season, and this was the title defining one of those games. Ian takes up the story."My vivid memory of the match was of 'Big' Dave Durie heading Blackpool into the lead in the second minute. Stan Matthews had a hand in the goal, literally! His throw in was flicked into the middle for Durie to nod home past Ray Wood. I remember thinking the boss would have been a bit put out by the marking if he had been present. Matthews never seemed to turn it on against us as Roger Byrne always gave him a hard time, marking him very closely. In this match though, he seemed to wander all over the pitch setting up chances for Bill Perry and Jackie Mudie, with one of his passes only being cut out by Duncan on the edge of the box. Our own outside right, Johnny Berry, was also our main danger but try as we did an equaliser would not come before half time"

It is fitting that Ian mentions Johnny Berry as if it was not for Stanley Matthews he would surely have been an England regular. Early in the second half a clash of heads between Tommy Taylor and Blackpool's Jackie Wright meant both had to go off for lengthy treatment. Ian takes up the second half story.

"When Tommy went off I thought our chance of sealing the title had gone, only for in the next attack, George Farm the Blackpool goalkeeper, to bring down John Doherty our inside right in the penalty area. Roger was our regular penalty taker but he had missed a couple and he passed the ball to Johnny Berry who gave Farm no chance for the equaliser. The two injured players came back on and typically Tommy Taylor was soon in the action, injured head and all. No doubt in my mind that Tommy was in the Tommy Lawton and Nat Lofthouse class as a header of the ball. A draw would have suited us more than Blackpool, but settling for such a result is not in the United mentality and we got the winner ten minutes from the end. Johnny Berry continued to have a great match and it was from one of his many crosses that Taylor, almost on his hands and knees, scrambled the ball home".

The teams for this memorable Manchester United match were;
United; WOOD, GREAVES, BYRNE, COLMAN, JONES, EDWARDS, BERRY, DOHERTY, TAYLOR, VIOLLET and PEGG.

Blackpool; FARM, FRITH, WRIGHT, KELLY (J) GRATRIX, KELLY (H), MATTHEWS, TAYLOR, DURIE, MUDIE, and PERRY.

In all Ian Greaves played 75 matches for Manchester United, including being the replacement for Roger Byrne at left back in the post Munich matches before a knee injury early in the 1959/60 season effectively ended his career. His management days at Huddersfield Town and Bolton Wanderers showed what a fine tactician he was. He sadly passed away in 2009 aged 76.

This victory over Blackpool sealed the League title for Manchester United, with the trophy being presented at the next home match against Portsmouth. I went to that game also, remembering it was a very wet afternoon with, surprisingly, a crowd of fewer than 40,000 present. It mattered not as the team that was shaking up the football world had won its first of what would surely be many honours, but how had this team which was the talk of football conceived by Matt Busby and his right hand man Jimmy Murphy, and now known as 'The Busby Babes' been built?

Chapter TWO
Arrival of Matt Busby

Old Trafford, Manchester, 11th March 1941
On one of its regular sorties over Manchester and Salford, the German Luftwaffe was naturally attracted to the Docks and Canal, which bordered the Trafford Park might of Engineering factories. One of the many bombs landed right on the Old Trafford ground, home of Manchester United knocking out its main stand, offices and dressing rooms. Having played Bury in a war time match the previous Saturday, it meant it would be another eight years before the first team of United would play there.

One of the clubs future greats, John Carey ,was incredibly passing in the aftermath, let him tell his story; "At the time I was working in the aircraft factory at Metro Vickers doing a twelve hour day with the management kindly letting me finish at mid day to play football in the afternoon. One day as I cycled into Trafford Park, a huge ball of fire hovered over the Old Trafford ground and, obviously, things were not looking good for the old place. The German bombers had managed to do what we had not done on the pitch-setting the place on fire!"

Cornbrook Old Trafford, Manchester, 19th February 1945
From his playing exploits with Manchester City and Liverpool and his native Scotland, Matt Busby was brought to a bombed out Old Trafford, even having to go to the Cornbrook offices of Chairman James Gibson to sign his contract. Gibson, the man who had saved the actual being of Manchester United in 1931, along with his trusted right hand man Walter Crickmer, as fine a secretary as any club could have, had earmarked Busby to take the team forward after the war. They had already started the MUJAC's before the start of that war and that move towards a young set of players was to become the mainstay of Busby's revolution. Amazingly, as I write this there has been a junior player in every Manchester United side since before the war.

Moving Forward; The FA Cup and League Title
One of Matt Busby's first moves was to secure a right hand man, and that was to be a former West Bromwich Albion and Wales star, Jimmy Murphy. Whilst Busby signed his contract on the above date in February 1945, it was actually October 1945 when he took over the reins of Manchester United. Other backroom staffs were required and Busby soon completed his team off the pitch. Besides Murphy, Bert Whalley, coming to the end of a fine career at United, was appointed as a coach, Ted Dalton as physio, Tom Curry 1st XI trainer, Bill Inglis 2nd XI trainer, Arthur Powell 'A' team and Bill Travis as 'B' team coach. There was also a little man who turned young players into big players for the club, Joe Armstrong who as scout was to find the budding stars who were to become the 'Busby Babes'. These names need to be recorded as men who developed truly great sides at Manchester United. What a future was in prospect for everyone

connected with the club, they were to start from scratch and to build a 'Theatre of Dreams'.

The club's other main job was to actually get themselves a ground to play on, and it was across the city to Maine Road and the home of neighbours Manchester City they went. A three year stay was to follow. An early sign of Matt Busby's Midas touch was shown when United won the Lancashire Cup Final, a competition clubs used to play their first team in, by beating Burnley 1-0 at Turf Moor thanks to a Jack Rowley goal. Later that year, the real football action was back as the replica of the short lived 1939/40 season was repeated with Grimsby Town starting the new 1946/47 season at Maine Road.

This was one of the most interesting league campaigns imaginable with official football slowly getting reorganised and attempting to deal with the problems which were springing up around every corner. Manchester United started with a 2-1 victory at the new surroundings of Maine Road before a crowd of 41,025 seeing the following side take the field; CROMPTON, CAREY, McGLEN, WARNER, CHILTON, COCKBURN, DELANEY, PEARSON, HANLON, ROWLEY and MITTEN. Goals came from Mitten and Rowley, with the only newcomer being an outside right signed from Glasgow Celtic for a steal at £4,000, Jimmy Delaney. He was to follow the likes of Billy Meredith and in later years such as Johnny Berry, George Best, Steve Coppell, Bryan Robson, David Beckham and Eric Cantona which made the shirt number seven iconic.

Keeping the number of seven going, that number of players from the Grimsby match, along with Delaney, was to become part of Matt Busby's first great Manchester United side. Jack Crompton was the steady goalkeeper all sides need, John Carey was Matt Busby's first great captain, Allenby Chilton was the rock at the heart of the defence, Henry Cockburn was the cheeky chappie wing half who became a massive favourite of the fans, Stan Pearson was a quite brilliant inside forward, Jack Rowley an explosive goal scoring centre forward, whilst Charlie Mitten was a complete outside left. With Delaney on the right wing, there were only two or three spots that needed completing for a perfect side.

How much would a centre forward who scored a goal every two games, capped by England, and also able to play in all the forward positions, be worth today? Jack Rowley was such a player and he was an integral part of Matt Busby's first great side. He felt, when I spoke to him in the early 1980's that Matt had a bit of good fortune though when he took over Manchester United. "I can't help think how lucky he was to take United over when he did. The players who were to achieve such success were all there, with the exception of Jimmy Delaney who came from Glasgow Celtic. No one player really stood out, the whole team seemed to fit like a glove; it was just one big family. Walter Crickmer and Tom Curry, who both tragically were killed in the Munich Air Disaster, were both a major reason for our success. Walter was the man who carried the club during the war, when he did everything in the running of the club, whilst Tom got the tremendously happy feeling in the team. The lads would do anything for him."

That first season back after the war, saw Manchester United finish as runners up to their Lancashire rivals Liverpool The reserves, playing Central League football under Jimmy Murphy, won their league but at the season end, Jimmy confided in Matt "There is not one reserve player who can step up to strengthen your league side".

"In that case" said Matt, "we will have to find and develop our own youngsters".

From those few words began the search to recruit the top schoolboy footballers from around Britain to Old Trafford.

By the 1947/48 season, Matt Busby had got his first XI in place. Johnny Aston slotted into the left back position, whilst the arrival of Johnny Morris after his demob to play inside right completed a star studded forward line of; Delaney, Morris, Rowley, Pearson and Mitten. This still stands the test of time and is right up there with any Manchester United forward line since. Matt Busby was now very happy with his first team, which again were runners up in 1948 but had the massive consolation of lifting the FA Cup by beating Blackpool 4-2 in a still remembered final for its quality and excitement.

Arsenal won the league this season, the match between them and United at Maine Road drew a crowd of 82,950 which is still the highest league crowd for an English football league game. With United playing at Maine Road, they effectively won the FA Cup by playing all their ties away from home. Aston Villa 6-4 in a memorable Villa Park tie, Liverpool 3-0 in a match played at Goodison Park, home of Everton ,Charlton Athletic 2-0 in a tie played at Huddersfield, both because Manchester City had first use of Maine Road, and then Preston North End 4-1 in a game United could play at Maine Road were all beaten before a semi final at Hillsborough, home of Sheffield Wednesday against Derby County, saw a Stan Pearson hat trick put United at Wembley Stadium for the first time and in a final for the first time since 1909.

The first major trophy of the Matt Busby era was achieved when United came from 1-2 behind to beat Blackpool, Stanley Matthews and all, 4-2 at Wembley. Two goals from Jack Rowley, one from Stan Pearson and a fourth United goal from the young right half Johnny Anderson sealed the victory for this great Manchester United side; CROMPTON, CAREY, ASTON, ANDERSON, CHILTON, COCKBURN, DELANEY, MORRIS, ROWLEY, PEARSON and MITTEN.

Over the next four years, Busby and Murphy set out their blue print for the long term future of Manchester United. They knew the side that had won the FA Cup was capable of another three or four season of success but then the whole team would virtually reach a finishing age at the same time. Under guidance from chief scout Joe Armstrong, Matt Busby and Jimmy Murphy travelled the length and breadth of Britain to secure young talent. Matt gave me an insight into this when I met him about a book I was doing. "The British Railway time table became my constant companion as I followed up scout's reports. Jimmy and I felt we were right at the front of this thinking so we did not want to waste our head start."

One position concerned Busby and that was goalkeeper. Jack Crompton was a loyal, dependable keeper but they say goalkeepers win you titles and in 1949 Matt went for an unexpected choice. He was a great admirer of Manchester City and England goalkeeper Frank Swift. This had been formed from a friendship when Busby played alongside Swift in the 1930's, indeed playing in FA Cup Finals together. When Frank Swift announced his retirement in 1949 Busby quickly moved to make him change his mind and become his number one. Unfortunately, City would not release his registration, Swift retired so Matt moved to sign Ray Wood from Darlington for £6,000 and when Jack Crompton succumbed to a wrist injury he was thrown into his debut away at St.James Park Newcastle to face his own idol Jackie Milburn, doing well as the teams drew 1-1. Ray Wood was actually the first of what became known as 'The Busby Babes' to make his debut. He became my hero when I first started watching United in 1953, mainly because in what seemed a grey world in those days, certainly where I lived in Salford, the colour of football shirts lifted young supporters, the separate colour of green worn by the goalkeepers being particularly memorable to a young lad. A year later Matt Busby moved to sign the Queens Park Rangers goalkeeper Reg Allen for £11,000. Reg Allen was a fantastic goalkeeper but £11,000 for a keeper was a fortune in those days and Reg was 31 years old. He also had suffered terribly in the war and this carried over, as it did for a lot of people. My own father, Albert, was a prisoner of war with the Japanese and I remember vividly his nightmares a good ten years after the end of that war. Allen was a player Busby had been involved with during war time matches, along with the young Ray Wood these two were deemed the future goalkeepers for Manchester United.

Other factors would also come into play for the new manager of Manchester United, one of them Busby's reticence to pay high wages. He felt, indeed through most of his time with the club, that playing for Manchester United was an honour, finance came second. This was despite the fact that United were attracting huge crowds to Maine Road whilst Old Trafford was waiting to be re built, crowds which in turn were producing high profits for the club. He also ruled the club like Sir Alex Ferguson did in his time by not standing for constant difference of opinions with players The first dispute was with Johnny Morris, who despite being a superb inside right felt he should explain his worth to Busby who soon had him out to Derby County for a £25,000 fee. Besides not wanting to over pay in wages, Matt Busby was also a very careful user of spending transfer money and it was with reluctance that he spent £20,000 of that Morris fee to recruit Johnny Downie from Bradford Park Avenue, then a league side and who had impressed Matt Busby when he had helped take United to a replay in the FA Cup. Another financial spat, this time with Charlie Mitten saw the popular outside left decide to take the riches of South America and take a lucrative contract in Bogota. Surprisingly, it was not an outside left that Busby bought, but an outside right in the diminutive Johnny Berry from Birmingham City. After the arrival of Berry, there would be only one major transfer at Manchester United for the next seven years that of the quite brilliant centre forward

Tommy Taylor, as the youth production line seamlessly rolled out not just good, but very good players for the club.

By the time Berry joined United, further runners up positions had been achieved in 1949, when the club had made its long awaited return to Old Trafford, and 1951 to make it four such positions in the five years since the war, along of course with the FA Cup. The team had started to evolve with the first young players coming through. Jeff Whitefoot was given his debut at Portsmouth in April 1950 and at 16 years and 105 days old he is still the youngest player to start a match for Manchester United, even though many accredit this to Duncan Edwards who was actually 16 years and 186 days on his debut. Mark Jones, a 17 year old centre half from Wombwell Barnsley made his debut in October 1950 at Old Trafford in a 3-1 victory over Sheffield Wednesday. Roger Byrne and Jackie Blanchflower both made their debuts at Anfield against a Liverpool side including Bob Paisley and Bill Liddell, helping United earn a 0-0 draw. Blanchflower was only 18, a Belfast lad whose brother, Danny, was already making his mark with Barnsley, later to lead Tottenham Hotspur to the elusive Cup and League double. Roger Byrne, then 22, was to become a true Manchester United legend. Although eventually finishing as both the Manchester United and England first choice left back, it was as outside left that he made most of his first Manchester United appearances.

Whilst the side was evolving on the pitch, there was the sad news in 1951 of the death of James Gibson, the chairman who had rescued Manchester United in 1931 financially, and brought Matt Busby to the club in 1945.He was replaced by Harold Hardman, who whilst a small man in stature had a very strong desire to succeed. As the 1951/52 season was underway it was clear this was going to be the last hurrah for a great Manchester United side, could they finish it with, finally, a league title?

One of the main reasons behind the constant performances since the war had been the leadership of Captain John Carey. He had been named Footballer of the year in 1949, the season after he had led United to the FA Cup. A man who played in virtually every shirt for the club, including goalkeeper once when Jack Crompton took ill just before a match at Sunderland. Carey did well in helping United earn a 2-2 draw in the North East He was a charming man, unaffected by his fame. I had the real pleasure of meeting him and recall one particular night at his home in Bramhall. The first thing that struck me was that you would not have known looking around how famous he was. The only sign indeed was the Footballer of the year statue. I had to ask had he any souvenirs so he went up stairs and brought down a supermarket type bag which contained some real footballing gems. There were shirts exchanged with Stanley Matthews, a starched white one with no markings but the number seven on its back. A Wales shirt worn by centre forward Trevor Ford which had the number nine boxed on its back, a green all Ireland shirt from when John captained the side and, finally, a light blue shirt with lacing across the neck from the Rest of Britain v Europe match in 1947 when John had captained the Rest side. I then asked him to take me through the end of the 1951/52 season when, finally, the League title returned to Manchester United, the first time since 1911 to Old Trafford.

"With all the near misses, I remember thinking to myself that after seven years it was about time I got myself a Championship medal. Season 1951/2 saw us up again near the top as we approached Easter. Victories over Burnley and Liverpool set the scene for the last two matches, both at home, against Chelsea and Arsenal, who themselves were in with a shout of the title. The Chelsea match was played on the Monday night, 21st April 1952, re arranged from the previous Saturday as Chelsea and Arsenal had played each other in the FA Cup semi final. No floodlights in those days so a tea time kick off, which explained the crowd being about 37,000. We just had to win and hope Arsenal did not beat West Bromwich Albion on the same night. Stan Pearson, a player incidentally I rated the finest I played alongside, scored early on which settled the nerves, then a really surprising thing happened, I scored! I did not get too many so when this ball bounced just right for me to belt home I just knew we were going to be champions".

John was too modest to say how much Manchester United fans loved him and they were delighted that this fantastic footballer had won the honour he had richly deserved. United went onto win this match 3-0 and with Arsenal failing to win it left the last match of the season, co incidentally between the two sides, mathematically impossible for Arsenal to lift the title. Back to that Chelsea match and John told me something which would just never, ever, be repeated.

"With it being an evening match by the time I had a couple of beers with the lads and having no car, I walked home to Chorlton. Walking most of the way with the fans it meant it was nearly 10 o'clock when I got in and the wife said as she was sorting the kids out could I do the washing up. So, there you have it, two hours after lifting the championship I was lifting the cups at home!"

The Manchester United side that night was; ALLEN, McNULTY, ASTON, CAREY, CHILTON, COCKBURN, BERRY, DOWNIE, ROWLEY, PEARSON and BYRNE. Six of this side had won the FA Cup four years earlier, and Jack Crompton was still around the club. Only two players, Allen and Berry had cost a fee, but both Matt Busby and Jimmy Murphy knew this was the end line for this side. It was a case of how soon the young players the scouting system had identified, and which Busby had brought from all corners to Old Trafford would develop. There was one lucky break in that around this time the FA introduced a new cup competition for the under 18's, called the FA Youth Cup. Busby decided this was to be the breeding ground for his new talent, and was prepared to give it a couple of years to make it work.

Chapter THREE

The Youngsters Start to Appear

From the 1952/53 season, Busby and Murphy had decided that the old guard were to be eased out and the new, young players, brought into the side. Ray Wood, Roger Byrne, Mark Jones, and Jackie Blanchflower had already joined the older Johnny Berry in the team, some for one off debuts others for longer spells. The season had started badly for the old guard, then the champions of England. Football was a big way of life for people in 1952, when over one million people attended football matches that season. Indeed, for the first Saturday of 1952/53 every one of the forty six football league matches drew crowds of over ten thousand except the fixtures at Barrow, Darlington and Rochdale.

In December 1952 Billy Foulkes, in a 2-1 victory at Liverpool, and David Pegg against Middlesbrough the week after, both made their Manchester United debuts. Foulkes was just shy of his 20th birthday, a miner in St.Helens he was hard as the rock he was breaking into down the pits. Pegg was only 17, a Doncaster lad but already an outstanding outside left. By the end of that season, Matt Busby had introduced 19 year old Dennis Viollet at Newcastle, Dennis a Manchester lad was a very talented inside left, both a maker and taker of goals. Like others at this time of their life he was doing his National Service. The week before an even younger player, 16 year old Duncan Edwards played at Old Trafford in a 1-4 defeat to Cardiff City. Duncan was sought after by many clubs, particularly Wolverhampton Wanderers who were close to his Dudley home, and like United preparing for the future by looking into a youth policy.

The search for players who could fit into the Manchester United framework, be part of a team whilst obviously having the ability to shine as a player, meant the club was searching all over Britain for talent. Indeed, two players who in later years were to join the club were asked to sign whilst still at school. Albert Quixall was spotted on a beach by Bert Whalley when he was on his holidays and he asked this blond haired young lad doing tricks on the beach whether he would like a trial at Old Trafford. Sadly, Quixall had already agreed to join Sheffield Wednesday. He later cost a British transfer fee to secure his services in the wake of Munich. A neighbour and school friend of Dennis Viollet was David Herd whose father Alec had played in the same Manchester City side as Matt Busby. He would have been a fine accusation alongside Viollet, but that had to wait another ten years as he was joining Arsenal. Whilst all of these players had started in United's youth and reserve sides, in March 1953, Matt Busby made his last foray into the transfer market for four years when he went over to Yorkshire to buy centre forward Tommy Taylor from second division Barnsley. They wanted a record breaking amount but to try and keep some of the pressure off, Busby agreed a figure of £29,999 and so, at the age of 21, Manchester United had a new hero to wear the famous red number nine shirt. He became known as the 'Smiling Executioner'.

The Busby Babes were nearly ready to play as the regular first team for Manchester United.

This same 1952/3 season had seen the start of the FA Youth Cup and its appropriate we look at the first couple of seasons which allowed young players to play competitive matches in readiness for wearing that famous red shirt.

Monday 4th May 1953
The FA Youth Cup Final 1st leg, Manchester United v Wolverhampton Wanderers
Forty Eight hours after the 1953 FA Cup Final at Wembley Stadium between Blackpool and Bolton Wanderers, where The Seasiders had won a still talked about match 4-3 thanks to the wizardry of Stanley Matthews and a hat trick from Stan Mortensen, the final of the newly created FA Youth Cup Final took place at Old Trafford between Manchester United and Wolverhampton Wanderers. This competition is devised to be a two legged affair for the semi and final. There had been talk of staging the final at Wembley, and sixty years or so on that is still a suggestion which this trophy would deserve.

It was no surprise that United and Wolves were the two sides involved in this match as both manager's, Matt Busby and Stan Cullis had shown the foresight to look to youth in the aftermath of the Second World War which had deprived lots of players seven years of their careers. The Manchester United side was to include five players who would be the basis of the forthcoming 'Busby Babes', Eddie Colman, Duncan Edwards, Liam (Billy) Whelan, David Pegg and Albert Scanlon. Whelan was an unknown name to the followers of United as he had been brought to the club as an urgent replacement for injured John Doherty at inside right. Doherty himself was a fine young player and this injury was doubly unfortunate as he not only missed playing in the final, but longer term Whelan was to become the Manchester United inside right as the team evolved into a brilliant young side.

Three of the Manchester United side had already played first team football, Edwards, Pegg and Eddie Lewis, who but for the signing of Tommy Taylor could possibly have had a longer career at Old Trafford. Lewis eventually played around twenty games for the club before joining Preston North End, onto West Ham United and then helping John Carey bring Leyton Orient into the First Division for their first and only time. One of my favourite players, Eddie Colman, was in the right half position and with Edwards formed a formidable half back pairing. On their way to this final, United had beat Leeds United 4-0 in their first ever Youth Cup, with a certain Jack Charlton playing for the Yorkshire side, with the next fixture non league Nantwich being no match for this fine young side, losing by the still record score of 23-0 at the United training ground, The Cliff in Salford with both David Pegg and Duncan Edwards scoring five each.

Wolves had not conceded a goal to reach the final stage, within five minutes they were a goal down! A great run down the left side by David Pegg left Noel McFarlane an easy goal from the outside right position. Wolves though had scored nearly thirty goals getting to this final and were level inside sixty seconds from their centre forward Smith. What turned out to be the ultimate difference was the sixteen year old lad from Dudley, a town close to Wolverhampton, but playing in the red shirt of Manchester United, Duncan Edwards. The England schoolboy international simply oozed confidence and class as he used his 12 stone frame to power across the pitch, marching through the smaller Wolverhampton side. Eddie Lewis headed United back in front with Scanlon doing the same to make it 3-1 after only fifteen minutes. By the same time inside the second half it was 6-1 to United, tie and final all over. McFarlane, Lewis and Pegg got those goals, before Billy Whelan scored his debut goal five minutes from the end to make the final score 7-1 to United, and this was a decent Wolves side! Nearly 21,000 fans witnessed this brilliant display and left knowing that, whilst it may take a couple of years, the next generation of Manchester United was on standby. A 2-2 draw at Molineux the following Saturday ensured a 9-3 aggregate victory for Manchester United and centre half Ronnie Cope lifting the first ever FA Youth Cup. There would be more, many more to follow... The Manchester United side for this final was; CLAYTON, FULTON, KENNEDY, COLMAN, COPE, EDWARDS, McFARLANE, WHELAN, LEWIS, PEGG and SCANLON.

This batch of Manchester United starlets were soon forming a major part of the Central League side monitored by Jimmy Murphy who also managed the youth team, although by the following season Duncan Edwards was to cement his place as a first team regular. Matt Busby knew this supply chain was flowing superbly, Bobby Charlton and Wilf McGuinness, England schoolboy Internationals were coming through to the Youth side in 1953/54 and when United travelled up to Kilmarnock to play a hastily arranged friendly under the Rugby Park lights in October 1953, the time for real change was at hand. The young players were given their heads in a 3-0 victory and from the next home match against Huddersfield Town there was now a 'new' Manchester United team on the pitch.

Reg Allen had real health issues in goal, and the time was now for Ray Wood with the loyal Jack Crompton captaining the Central League team nurturing the youngsters coming through. Billy Foulkes and Roger Byrne were now the regular full backs as John Carey was moving into management and Johnny Aston, like Allen, suffering from health problems. The right half spot was one Busby had never really covered, surprising as that was the position he had filled with credit in his own playing days. He knew Eddie Colman was going to solve all his problems and was willing to wait another year till he was really ready. Allenby Chilton would be allowed to join Grimsby Town as player manager letting Mark Jones take the number five shirt the following season and with Duncan Edwards now ready to be the number six Henry Cockburn's fine career at Old Trafford was coming to an end. Stan Pearson goes down as a Manchester United great and Matt Busby allowed both him and Cockburn to join local side Bury with Dennis Viollet stepping into the number ten shirt. Johnny Berry was now the regular outside right with Jimmy Delaney having returned to Scotland. Inside him was, like the right half position, one

Matt Busby had not really cemented after Morris moved to Derby, although Johnny Downie had been an adequate stand in. Busby knew though that in young players such as Whelan and even younger Charlton that place would be filled soon. It was suspected that Busby made a move for the Hibernian and Scotland player Bobby Johnstone, part of the famous five Hibernian forward line, but Bobby went to the other Manchester side, City, and had a decent career with them winning the FA Cup in 1956. Tommy Taylor was already confirming the club's hopes of him being a top class centre forward, and he soon linked brilliantly with Dennis Viollet. This just left the outside left position and Busby had two candidates in youngsters Pegg and Scanlon to replace Jack Rowley when he, like Chilton took up a player manager role, Rowley at Plymouth Argyle. Matt Busby's 'Babes' were in position...

The 1953/54 FA Youth Cup followed a similar pattern to the first season's competition with both United and Wolves sailing through to the final. Whilst Colman, Edwards Scanlon and Pegg were still eligible to play, as I mentioned earlier, they had been joined by two other young stars of the future. Manchester boy Wilf McGuinness, the England schoolboy captain was an all action left half, and a young lad from the mining North East town of Ashington, an England team mate of Wilf's, Bobby Charlton who was in the side at centre forward. Wolves again played the first leg at Old Trafford but this time it was them who dominated the first half going at one point into a 3-1 lead before United fought back to draw level at 4-4.

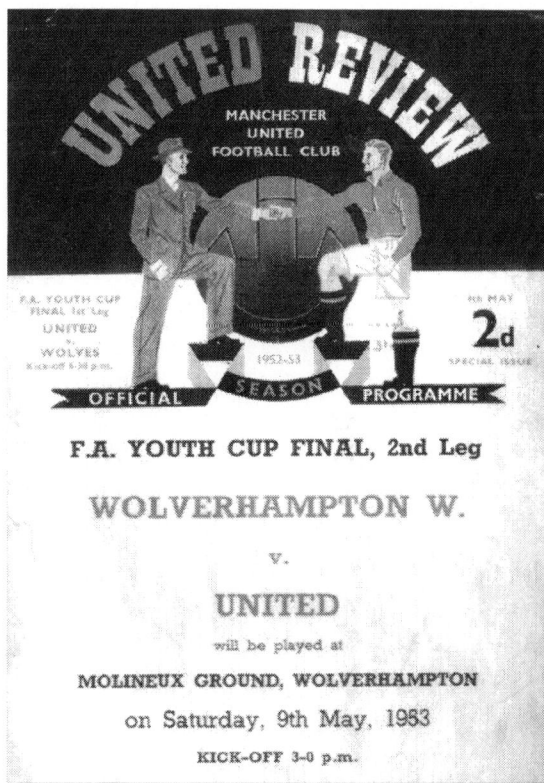

F.A. YOUTH CUP FINAL, 2nd Leg

WOLVERHAMPTON W.

v.

UNITED

will be played at

MOLINEUX GROUND, WOLVERHAMPTON

on Saturday, 9th May, 1953

KICK-OFF 3-0 p.m.

Molineux this time was expecting to see their side lift the trophy and over 28,000 turned up for the coronation. Matt Busby's youngsters though were not prepared to release their trophy and a David Pegg penalty won the tie and saw him lift the FA Youth Cup for the second successive season for Manchester United.

Chapter FOUR

Preparing for the Glory Years

Matt Busby was so confident of what he had coming through the Manchester United conveyor belt he felt comfortable in telling the clubs shareholders that despite lifting the championship in 1952, after a string of runner up positions, along with lifting the FA Cup in 1948 plus seeing the club back in its rightful home of Old Trafford, that he felt the youngsters had to be given their chance or the clubs future would leave no optimism. Even so, and despite winning the new FA Youth cup in its first two seasons of 1953 and 1954, that future needed to be delivered as the start of the 1954/55 season commenced.

A 1-3 home defeat to Portsmouth was not the start of delivering glory! It did not help that the Manchester sky's opened and there was torrential rain which actually nearly caused abandonment at half time. The team that started the season 1954/55 against Portsmouth before a very wet Old Trafford crowd of 38,203 was; WOOD, FOULKES, BYRNE, WHITEFOOT, CHILTON, EDWARDS, BERRY, BLANCHFLOWER, WEBSTER, VIOLLET and ROWLEY. The average age of this side was 24, although Chilton at 35 and Rowley at 33 kept it much higher than it would be in the future. Rowley indeed was the United goal scorer in the match which saw Colin Webster replace the injured Tommy Taylor at centre forward. Webster had joined United on a free from Cardiff City a couple of seasons before, on the recommendation of Dennis Viollet who played alongside him as they served their National Service together.

Two days later the same United side won 4-2 at Hillsborough against Sheffield Wednesday and then repeated it at Bloomfield Road against Blackpool to make it a high scoring start to the new season despite the loss of Taylor. When they won two home matches inside a week at Old Trafford against Sheffield Wednesday in the return fixture, and against Charlton Athletic, it was a great start to that season. Tommy Taylor made his season debut against Charlton, scoring in a 3-1 victory, which was also United's first change which saw them win four out of the first five fixtures.

A great victory at White Hart Lane against Tottenham Hotspur by 2-0 was followed by a satisfactory 1-1 draw away at bogey side Bolton Wanderers. That same score was repeated at Old Trafford against Huddersfield Town a few days after United had recorded their second double of the season by beating Tottenham Hotspur 2-0 which saw a marvellous points haul, from a very settled side after the first nine matches. Indeed, the only change had seen Taylor and Webster rotate the centre forward position, both scoring goals when they played.

It is interesting looking at the match programme against Huddersfield to see how Matt Busby saw the opening part of the season. He commented; "It has frequently been urged that the blend of youth and experience is the ideal partnership in football. Well, I would like to pay tribute to the consistency and good form of the two oldest players in the side, Allenby Chilton and Jack Rowley" This recognition of the influence the last two survivors from the 1948 FA Cup winning side playing at first team level was having on his new, younger stars of the future was also reflected at the Central League side as well where another two of that cup winning side, Jack Crompton and Henry Cockburn, were passing their advice on to even younger United starlets. Jimmy Murphy was playing a vital role at this level , managing the Central League team giving his young charges all of his experience, cajoling them along, knowing who to be hard on who to put an arm around. His contribution to Manchester United must never be forgotten...

Manchester United had a further three sides playing at junior level ,the 'A' and 'B' sides playing in the Manchester League and the Lancashire League with their fixtures being played at The Cliff training ground, and a Junior team participating in the Altrincham Junior League with their fixtures being played at Wilbraham Road.

Looking back at a recent Saturday's fixtures, that match programme against Huddersfield informed that such as Geoff Bent, Freddie Goodwin, Ronnie Cope and Albert Scanlon played in the 'A' team match, with Eddie Colman and Bobby Charlton in the 'B' side. Interestingly, Shay Brennan and Kenny Morgans were in the junior's side that day. Of the thirteen matches these young sides had played so far this season they had won eleven and drawn the other two.

A real test for the new young Manchester United players came with three away matches inside a week, two of them league fixtures, at local rivals Manchester City the other at the side they were vying with at the top of the table, Wolverhampton Wanderers, along with a friendly at Clyde when Matt Busby took his young side up to Scotland for an early season break. The City match ended the teams stay at the top of the table when they lost 3-2, with Don Gibson replacing Jeff Whitefoot in the team at right half. Don Gibson was an interesting player who caused Matt Busby a decision to make as he also had married his daughter Sheena and he did not want complaints of nepotism being aired. The friendly at Clyde saw a further defeat, this time by 4-1 although in defence of United, four of their players were away training with the national England and Northern Ireland sides. It will be hard to believe nowadays to think that the following Saturday when the two sides at the top of the table, Wolverhampton Wanderers and Manchester United met at Molineux, the four players, Ray Wood, Bill Foulkes and Roger Byrne for England and Jackie Blanchflower for Northern Ireland were absent! It was, therefore, not as much a surprise to see United go down 4-2 on the day that Ian Greaves and Paddy Kennedy made their United debuts and Henry Cockburn played his last match for the club before joining Bury. Cockburn was a brilliant Manchester United player and he joined his old team mate Stan Pearson at Gigg Lane.

Continuing the hard to imagine happenings for younger fans today, when United returned to Old Trafford to play Cardiff City, the editor of the famous club programme the 'United Review' Sidney F. Wicks informed that on the weekend of the recent City match he had gone to the Cotswolds for the weekend and due to no radio or even

Sunday morning newspapers it was lunch time on the Sunday before he found out the score from Maine Road. Oh the days before Sky sports, texting, twitter and regular telephone communications around the quieter areas of the country! Tommy Taylor, a man many thought unlucky not to have been in the England side the week before, although early season injuries had not helped, scored four goals as United returned to winning ways by beating Cardiff 5-2.

Whilst seven goals in a match was high scoring, the week after Cardiff's visit United went to Stamford Bridge to face one of the surprise sides Chelsea, and came away with the better of an eleven goal bonanza. Chelsea was drawing the crowds to see their exciting side and 56,000 came along fully expecting another victory. They went away marvelling at the play of Matt Busby's youngsters with a hat trick from Dennis Viollet, two more from Tommy Taylor and one from Jackie Blanchflower sealing an amazing 6-5 United victory, having been 5-2 up at one stage.

Old Trafford was still not seeing the crowds this young side deserved with only 29,000 watching a 2-2 draw with Newcastle before Goodison Park was packed out with over 63,000 going home happy as they saw Everton win 4-2. Matt Busby was keeping faith with a very settled side and they responded with a 2-1 home victory over Preston North End before suffering their fifth consecutive away defeat, this time 3-0 at Sheffield United's Bramall Lane ground, then still also the home of Yorkshire County Cricket Club.

Keeping a cricket theme going, the week after when Arsenal visited Old Trafford, Freddie Goodwin made his United debut replacing the injured Duncan Edwards. Goodwin was also a Lancashire cricketer and he was joined by another debutant, Albert Scanlon who replaced Jack Rowley as United got back onto winning ways with a 2-1 victory. The pair of them had actually played mid week at Hibernian as Matt Busby took his ever developing young side back to Scotland for another friendly. This time they had a better result than at Clyde and beat the side who would win the Scottish League this season 3-1. The 'United Review' for the Arsenal match recorded the incredible feats of the younger Manchester United sides. The FA Youth side had beaten Manchester City at Maine Road 2-1 with Duncan Edwards scoring both from the centre forward position, as they embarked on the third defence of the trophy, whilst the 'A', 'B' and junior side were all still undefeated. In all at that time they had played a total of 40 matches winning 37 and drawing the other three.

Following a sixth consecutive away defeat, this time 2-0 at West Bromwich Albion, United had slipped to fifth position in the table. The yo-yo displays continued when newly promoted Leicester City visited Old Trafford. A 3-1 victory saw Jack Rowley return to the side with two goals, whilst his free scoring brother, Arthur, scored Leicester's goal. Former United favourite, Johnny Morris was also in the Leicester side. A very disappointing crowd of 19,369 was at Old Trafford, which after the massive crowds at recent away matches at Chelsea and Everton was a real concern.

Finally the away losses were rectified at Turf Moor with a 4-2 victory thanks to a Colin Webster hat trick as he again was a very competent replacement for the injured Tommy Taylor. A very fine left back, Geoff Bent, made his debut for United in this match. A Salford lad, Bent was to prove a more than adequate deputy for Roger Byrne, indeed he probably would have been a first choice at most clubs. Duncan Edwards also missed this match as he was playing for the youth side as they continued in the competition with the same score line as the first team, 4-2 at Barnsley. Confirming a return to better away performances, a 0-0 draw at Fratton Park, home of Portsmouth, was more than satisfactory as the Christmas fixtures loomed. Sadly, a double defeat to Aston Villa 0-1 at Old Trafford and 2-1 at Villa Park made it a disappointing time for Manchester United fans as 1955 appeared on the horizon.

1955 did bring an immediate response as 51,000 Manchester United fans came to Old Trafford and backed Matt Busby's growing side, being rewarded with a convincing 4-1 victory over Blackpool. Nineteen year old David Pegg made another appearance as deputy to Jack Rowley, although this was his thirty second game for United, showing how these young players were gaining experience very rapidly. To compare what Pegg was like think a young Ryan Giggs, a lively outside left beating full backs for fun, a maker and taker of goals.

The FA Cup brought a visit to third division Reading and a full house at Elm Park. They nearly saw a giant killing as United were holding on at the end to a 1-1 draw thanks to another Colin Webster goal. When Webster got two of United's goals in a 4-1 replay victory, he had scored eleven goals in thirteen matches this season, a very tidy return. Tommy Taylor had scored thirteen goals from his fifteen matches at this stage of the season.

As winter arrived the weather turned very cold with snow causing the postponement of the away match at The Valley, the cavernous home of Charlton Athletic. Old Trafford was not hit as bad and the reserves managed to play their fixture with Blackburn Rovers, a 5-0 victory putting Jimmy Murphy's side equal top of the table. Jack Crompton was the steady hand on the young shoulders, which included future stars such as Geoff Bent, Mark Jones, Billy Whelan and David Pegg. Blackburn also had stars of the future in their side, Roy Vernon and Bryan Douglas being two future Internationals. The week after Tommy Taylor returned from his injury problems and promptly got back onto the score sheet as United drew 1-1 against Bolton Wanderers at Old Trafford.

A welcome 3-1 away victory at Huddersfield Town was played on a date that would, in three years time, be immortalised in Manchester United's history, the 5th February. In 1955 this was a match at Huddersfield, three years on it would be the last fixture played by the Busby Babes in Belgrade against Red Star...

Two meetings in successive weeks against local rivals Manchester City followed, one in the 4th round of the FA Cup, the other in a league fixture. That took place at Old Trafford and in one of the great 'derby' shocks, City won 5-0.United, despite being without Tommy Taylor (yet again) and Dennis Viollet, were totally outplayed by a City side which was perfecting the new Revie system which involved Don Revie playing in a deep lying centre forward position as the Hungarians had perfected in their two hammerings of England in the past eighteen months. The week after, a full house at Maine Road of 75,000 saw the sides meet again with the sending off of Allenby Chilton not helping matters as City recorded their third victory over United in the season, this time 2-0 as they moved forward to eventually contest the Final at Wembley against Newcastle United.

This was to be a pivotal few days for Manchester United as the two remaining 'old' stagers from the 1948 and 1952 trophy winning sides played their last games for the club. The cup defeat at Maine Road was the last game for Jack Rowley ending a marvellous career, full of goals a genuine top class player, whether that be as centre forward or on the left wing. The Wednesday after the cup defeat at Maine Road, Allenby Chilton was to play his last Manchester United game. This was against Wolverhampton Wanderers at Old Trafford in a re arranged mid week fixture. A 2-4 defeat was not the memory Chilton would have wanted to leave but, like Rowley, he was a marvellous United player. Six foot tall built like a brick out house, he dominated the Manchester United defence for many years. Chilton and Rowley played over 800 appearances for the club, they were main stays of United winning the FA Cup and League Championship, but just as importantly, they were there to show Matt Busby's young players what was expected of them from the club. Both players went onto management, Jack with Plymouth Argyle and Allenby with Grimsby Town.

Mark Jones now had the opportunity to move up and become the regular Manchester United centre half. He was a player all his team mates appreciated, calm, pipe smoking, determined, he possessed all the attributes needed from a number five. David Pegg was also given the chance to become the United outside left and their inclusion away at Cardiff City brought the average age of the team down to 22. Not the start hoped for though as Cardiff won 3-0.

A goal from Duncan Edwards defeated Burnley at Old Trafford, the week after he was playing centre half for the youth side as Jack Rowley's new side, Plymouth Argyle visited Old Trafford in the FA Youth cup. I went to the match which was played at 11 in the Saturday morning with a reserve fixture against Everton following at 2.15pm. Plymouth were no match for a quite brilliant United youth team, not only having Edwards in the side but also Eddie Colman, Wilf McGuinness, Shay Brennan and Bobby Charlton. The last two both scored hat tricks as United won 9-0. I stayed on to watch the reserves beat Everton 2-0 keeping them in second place in the table. The first team played a friendly at Lincoln that day with Billy Whelan making his debut in a 3-2 victory.

A surprise 1-2 home defeat to Everton kept United fifth, but Matt Busby's side was now full of his future young stars and they responded with a fine 2-0 victory at Preston North

End, with Billy Whelan making his First Division full debut for United, the sixth player following Greaves, Kennedy, Goodwin, Bent and Scanlon in doing so this season.

Two years after his Manchester United debut, and still only eighteen years old, Duncan Edwards made his International debut on 2nd April 1955 at Wembley Stadium against Scotland. He joined his club mate Roger Byrne as England demolished 'The Auld Enemy' 7-2. A future Manchester United manager Tommy Docherty, was in the Scotland side that day. Back at Old Trafford Manchester United played Sheffield United without two key players and scored an emphatic victory 5-0 with Billy Whelan scoring his first senior goal. Geoff Bent came into the side for Byrne making his second United appearance.

Easter saw the usual busy period in those days of three matches in four days. Sadly for United, defeats on Good Friday at Sunderland 4-3 and at Filbert St Leicester the day after by a single goal meant they were marooned in seventh position. The Easter Monday Old Trafford crowd at least saw a 2-2 draw in the Sunderland return match. The reserves were now in third place in the Central League whilst the junior sides at this stage of the season had played a total of 73 matches, losing three and drawing three, winning the other 67! The next batch of Busby's Babes were preparing well.

Duncan Edwards continued his memorable month of April by playing in the semi finals of the FA Youth cup against Chelsea. He scored all United goals as they won 2-1 at Old Trafford and at Stamford Bridge. Due to these matches Edwards missed the 3-0 victory over West Bromwich Albion and the mid week 2-0 defeat at cup finalists Newcastle United, but was back for when London had its first real sight of the 'Busby Babes' as a side. Nine of that eventual squad played at Highbury as United turned on all the style to beat Arsenal 3-2. London had a quick second sight as United drew 1-1 at The Valley in the re arranged match with Charlton Athletic.

A third London side, this time the new champions Chelsea, for the first time in their history, visited Old Trafford for the last game of the season. I went to the match on 30th April 1955 with my father Albert, joining a crowd of 34,933. This brought the season average to 34,077 which held up well against the National average of 32,656. On this final match we went to the Stretford End, again climbing those many stairs to reach the top banking. Whilst the actual match does not live long in my memory what happened after does! Manchester United beat the champions 2-1 to record a famous season double and give notice that Matt Busby's young side was now really ready to compete further up the league than the fifth position they would finish. Albert Scanlon and Tommy Taylor got the United goals but as the match ended my dad suggested we went around to the old players entrance which was then where the Munich tunnel is now. He knew I had brought my autograph book with me and as the Chelsea side came out to get on their coach he said wait here a minute and promptly got on with them! Next minute the coach starts up and moves along the way towards the concourse with my dad on it. What do I as an eight year old tell my mother where my dad has gone! Anyhow, as it reached the top road he suddenly was let off and proudly handed me back my book with all the Chelsea players autographs in it. Sadly, of course, over the years it went missing but what would those be worth today, particularly as it took Chelsea over another fifty years to win the league again. The Manchester United side this last game of the season was; WOOD, FOULKES, BYRNE, GIBSON, JONES, GOODWIN, BERRY, BLANCHFLOWER, TAYLOR, VIOLLET and SCANLON. Duncan Edwards was playing in the second leg of the FA Youth Cup final at West Bromwich Albion, whilst this turned out to be Don Gibson's last match for United, he was transferred to Sheffield Wednesday in the summer. Mark Jones and David Pegg had come in for Chilton and Rowley who had moved onto management, whilst Tommy Taylor was now fully fit from his persistent ankle injuries to be the regular centre forward.

For the third successive season the youth team lifted the FA Youth cup after a 7-1 aggregate victory over West Bromwich Albion, who had Maurice Setters in their side. In the United side those games were Bobby Charlton, Shay Brennan, Wilf McGuinness, captain Eddie Colman and of course Duncan Edwards. The first team finished fifth, the reserves were runners up whilst all three junior sides won their respective leagues with the 'A' team and junior side BOTH scoring over 200 goals in the season. One interesting player in the 'A' side who does not often get a mention in talk about Manchester United was the centre forward Laurie Cassidy. Whilst this side was full of aspiring Manchester United players for the future, Laurie by 1955 was 32 year old but in another life was a well respected Head teacher in

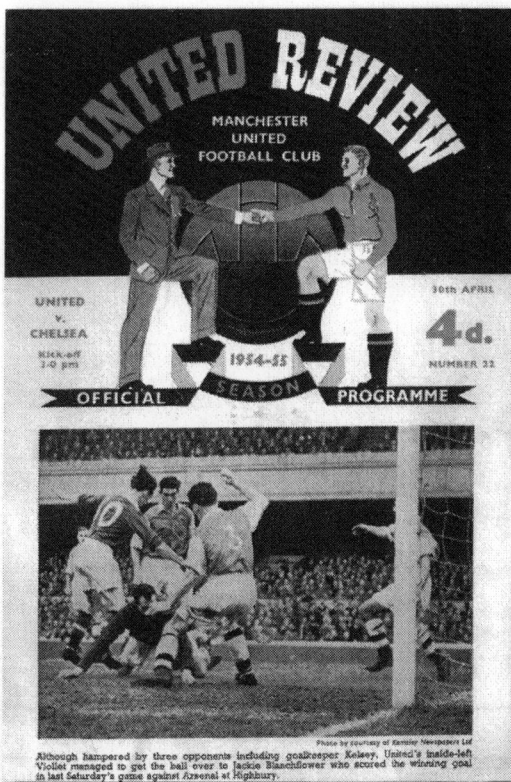

Although hampered by three opponents including goalkeeper Kelsey, United's inside-left Viollet managed to get the ball over to Jackie Blanchflower who scored the winning goal in last Saturday's game against Arsenal at Highbury.

Manchester, ran Manchester schoolboy's football team and helped with the England schoolboy side. He also was instrumental in helping Nobby Stiles and Brian Kidd land at Old Trafford. During this particular season as the over age player, Laurie Cassidy scored over 60 goals himself. A man who did a lot for Manchester United.

Manchester United went on a post season tour of Scandinavia winning all four matches, three in Denmark and one in Sweden. The Busby Babes were now in place to show England, then all of Europe, what a great side they would be...

Chapter FIVE

A Champions Diary, Part One

1955/56 saw Manchester United win the League Championship, the Central League and the FA Youth Cup for the fourth time in a row. Let us look through that season, starting with the months of August 1955 to December 1955 as a weekly diary of events for the teams that wore the colours of Manchester United.

August 1955

Matt Busby welcomed his bright, young, exciting side back for pre season at The Firs Fallowfield fully expecting that this would be the year transition would become reality.

Their first encounter would be with newly promoted Birmingham City at their St Andrews ground. This was always going to be a tester but Matt Busby found himself with a major problem when winger Johnny Berry, an ex Birmingham City player, limped into Old Trafford just before the side was due to leave for the West Midlands, with a badly swollen ankle suffered in a loosening up training session the day before. United were, therefore, forced to make this late change bringing in the versatile Welshman Colin Webster, who had been left out of all United sides due to an expected fifteen day army training exercise in Chester.

Birmingham, as were to be expected, were roared on by a capacity 38,000 crowd giving full vent to their anthem 'Keep right onto the end of the road'. With Johnny Berry absent, captain Roger Byrne was the oldest player in the side which had an average age of 22. The home side had the better of the opening half hour which was not helped by Tommy Taylor pulling a thigh muscle to see him a virtual passenger on the right wing with Webster switching to centre forward. Dennis Viollet was in fine form though and his two quality goals, which Birmingham pulled back each time to equalise, ensured a decent draw. Ray Wood had to be in fine form to ensure the point returned to Old Trafford. Incidentally, not one of Manchester United's side had appeared at St Andrews in a losing sixth round FA Cup tie 1-0 in 1951, a period which had seen Matt Busby overall his side from FA Cup and League Champions to another tilt at the title. The side on this opening day was; WOOD, FOULKES, BRYNE, WHITEFOOT, JONES, EDWARDS, WEBSTER, BLANCHFLOWER, TAYLOR, VIOLLET and SCANLON.

On the same day United's reserve side, captained by Jack Crompton, started the season with a Old Trafford game against Derby County. Even younger players, including Youth Cup winners, Bent, McGuinness, Whelan, and Pegg were coming through the system, which ensured a winning start 4-2. Lower down the scale the 'A' side beat Bury 9-2 with a hat trick from Bobby Charlton earning him a promotion to the reserve side for the following match.

Midweek Tottenham Hotspur visited Old Trafford for a 6.30pm kick off due to still no floodlights, with the Blanchflower brothers opposing themselves. Jackie was again at inside forward, with his brother Danny playing right half for Tottenham. Jackie though, was not tied to one position, he was a very versatile player and appeared at centre half, centre forward and inside forward for United, and on one memorable day eighteen months on he was a replacement goalkeeper in an FA Cup Final. Johnny Berry returned to outside right with Colin Webster moving into centre forward due to Tommy Taylor's injury. Both these players were to be the United goal scorers as for the second match running Manchester United were held to a 2-2 draw. The same evening the reserves went to Barnsley and came away with a 2-0 victory.

West Bromwich Albion visited Old Trafford the following Saturday, without their star centre forward Ronnie Allen. He was always a hero to me, a diminutive player who had first fired my imagination playing in the first FA Cup final I saw via a large box, small screen TV, the 1954 match between Albion and Preston North End which Albion won 3-2. Johnny Berry was again unfit so Webster returned to outside right and another of Busby's young players, Eddie Lewis a Youth Cup winner in 1953, being brought into the side at centre forward. He also got onto the score sheet, along with Viollet and Scanlon to give United their first victory of the season by 3-1.Today of course, fans of Manchester United are used to seeing full house crowds of 75,000 regularly filling the Old Trafford stadium, back in 1955 for this first Saturday of the season, 31,996 were present, that an increase of the previous Wednesday's 25,406. A visit to St James Park Newcastle for the reserve side brought a third victory out of three with another 2-0 victory.

The reserves had a quick turnaround as they were to play Barnsley in the return fixture at Old Trafford forty eight hours after. They were playing some magnificent football and totally overwhelmed Barnsley by winning 7-1, fifteen goals for in four matches played. For the last fixture in the month of August 1955, United's first team travelled to White Hart Lane to play a quick return fixture with Tottenham Hotspur. Another injury, this time to inside forward Dennis Viollet, meant Duncan Edwards had to show his real versatility by moving forward into the number ten shirt with Freddie Goodwin stepping in at six. His class for such a young player was there for all to see as he not only changed position he scored both United goals as they achieved a fine victory by 2-1.

September 1955

A new month brought a visit across town to play local rivals City. It was starting to feel that some sort of hoodoo was beginning to be created in City's favour when after being out played for the first half hour, City went up the other end and scored what proved to be the winner. In the second half though it took a another fine display from goalkeeper Ray Wood to keep United in the match with Duncan Edwards unable to repeat his White Hart Lane exploits as he continued at inside left. The news from Old Trafford though from the 'mini derby' gave the good information that United's reserves had again gone on a goal spree beating City 6-2 to remain unbeaten at the top of the Central League.

The cost of watching football in 1955 at Old Trafford was reported in the club programme, the 'United Review' for the mid week home match with Everton,with the information that ground price was 2/- (10p) unreserved seating 5/- (25p) with reserved seating being 6/6 (33p) Then Old Trafford had a massive open section behind the Stretford End, the United Road paddock having a part cover and then another open end behind the goal where the scoreboard was at the back. Along the main stand, the railway line side, was the only seating with the sides coming out of a tunnel at the half way line. Everton had not started the season too well and against a still a depleted United side due to injuries, United still defeated them 2-1 with Duncan Edwards providing a goal alongside one from Jackie Blanchflower.

A second successive single goal away defeat, this time at Sheffield United, may not have set all the alarm bells ringing but the injury and illness situation certainly did. Already without Taylor and Viollet, a further re shuffle had to take place when Duncan Edwards dropped out with a sudden attack of flu. This meant call ups for young forwards David Pegg and Billy Whelan, but not surprisingly, the attack never found any sort of rhythm. The defence had performed admirably all season, therefore, it was extremely tough luck on Mark Jones, who had proved such a giant at centre half, that he should have the unlucky experience of conceding a late own goal which settled the match by misfiring a back pass which gave goalkeeper Ray Wood no chance of stopping. Interestingly, Sheffield United's manager was Joe Mercer and he accompanied the United team to Old Trafford on his way home to Hoylake. Could you have imagined Sir Alec Ferguson giving Arsene Wenger a lift?! At Old Trafford the reserves dropped their first point when Sheffield United held them to a 1-1 draw. Tommy Taylor made a welcome return from his opening day injury for the reserves and scored the United goal.

Taylor was still not considered fit enough to return for the mid week return with Everton at Goodison Park. Indeed, yet another player dropped out when Jeff Whitefoot was unfit and it gave Walter Whitehurst his first, and what turned out to be his last, match for the club. After beating Everton a week earlier, and leading this match 2-1 at half time, the wheels came off and Everton ran out comfortable victors 4-2. Thankfully, this was to turn out to be the low point for the team this season as, finally, Matt Busby was able to get his preferred first team out.

Walter Whitehurst was back in the reserve side on the Saturday as they travelled to Deepdale to face Preston North End and continued their unbeaten run by holding out for a 0-0 draw. Forty miles down the A6 back in Manchester the first team resembled the side Busby wanted with the return of Taylor and Viollet and they both responded with a goal which with another from Pegg won the match 3-2 against a Preston side which had Tommy Docherty at right half and the quite brilliant Tom Finney at outside right. In my opinion Finney was the best non Manchester United footballer I have seen. He could play in all FIVE forward positions, top class on either wing or a very good centre forward. Interestingly in this period of time, football clubs were able to keep their star player with the transfer market not really a regular occurrence. Nearly every side had its own star, a man who was the hero of that particular town or city. Others that come to mind such as Tom Finney at Preston were; Stanley Matthews at Blackpool, Nat

Lofthouse at Bolton, Jimmy McIlroy at Burnley, Billy Wright at Wolverhampton Wanderers, Roy Bentley at Chelsea, Jackie Milburn at Newcastle, Roy Paul at Manchester City, Jimmy Dickinson at Portsmouth and Ronnie Allen at West Bromwich Albion.

Mid week the reserves went to Goodison Park to play their fixture with Everton and returned to winning ways to extend their lead at the top of the table. They won 2-1 with the goals coming from Billy Whelan and Bobby Charlton, with Wilf McGuinness, Geoff Bent, John Doherty and Albert Scanlon also in the team. A young, strong Scotsman from Aberdeen, made his debut in this match, Alex Dawson who was a natural goal scorer. When they returned to Old Trafford on the Saturday, the reserves hammered Burnley 7-1 with Whelan and Charlton again amongst the goals. Across Lancashire the first team's played out a goalless draw at Turf Moor. United looked a much stronger side now with the injured players returning, although Dennis Viollet suffered a knock in this match which made him a virtual passenger on the wing, no substitutes in those days of course.

Matt Busby took his side back to Scotland for a friendly at Hibernian who had become the first British club to compete in the new European Cup this season. Chelsea being dissuaded from competing by our Football Association. There is always a warm welcome to Manchester United when they go to play in Scotland and this visit did not lose them any friends even though Hibernian won easily 5-0 under the Easter Road floodlights. United though were far from full strength with Edwards, Berry, Taylor and Viollet not travelling. When Colin Webster went down with flu on the morning of the match, young Johnny Scott had to make a six hour car journey to Edinburgh to take his place on the right wing.

October 1955
Luton Town's first ever First Division match at Old Trafford drew a crowd of 34,409 to see Tommy Taylor get amongst the goals with two and Colin Webster, in for the injured Viollet, also on the score sheet. Matt Busby liked to cultivate team spirit and with a flu bug around took the side to Blackpool staying at his favourite hotel there the Norbreck before this Luton match. Another youngster, Geoff Bent, stepped into the side as a replacement for Roger Byrne who was playing for England in a World Cup tie against Denmark in Copenhagen the following day. This victory put United in fourth place two points behind leaders Blackpool. The reserves travelled over The Pennines to play Leeds United with a hat trick from Billy Whelan and a goal from Bobby Charlton bringing a deserved 4-0 victory, another two points and a clear lead at the top of their league. Eddie Colman made his reserve debut at Leeds.

A lot of friendly fixtures get swept under the carpet but one significant one for Manchester United followers arrived on Tuesday 4th October 1955 when Matt Busby took his side up the A56 to play neighbours Bury in a friendly. That was where two of Busby's favourite players, Stan Pearson and Henry Cockburn had gone to play out their fantastic careers. It was a youngster making his first appearance with a Manchester United senior side though who caught the eye, Bobby Charlton. After scoring nine goals in nine appearances for the reserves, a crowd of nearly 9,000 saw him score one of United's goals as they won 5-1.

In the 1950's one of the most famous clubs were Wolverhampton Wanderers. They had been champions and runners up the previous two seasons and rated as a top attraction to all grounds. The only foreign influence in the game in the 1950's was the advent of continental floodlight friendlies and Wolves were right at the forefront in this venture. Games with star sides from Russia and Hungary had excited the soccer masses. In the Wolves side were lots of England Internationals, captain Billy Wright, goalkeeper Bert Williams, wing half Bill Slater, inside forward Dennis Wilshaw and wingers Johnny Hancocks and Jimmy Mullen and they were expected to give Matt Busby's emerging side a real test. With Duncan Edwards still unwell, Matt Busby gave a debut to local Manchester lad Wilf McGuinness, who of course 15 years later was to become Manchester United manager. Wilf also became a brilliant after dinner speaker and he told a story of his debut match. "Jimmy Murphy was a great motivator and when he told me Matt was going to give me my debut against Wolves he said remember the inside forward you were going to face, Peter Broadbent, was trying to steal your win bonus, money I was going to give to my mother. I tore into Peter, who is a lovely bloke by the way, kicking him up hill and down dale" The attraction of Wolverhampton Wanderers was reflected in a gate of 48,638 who witnessed a seven goal thriller, Wolves twice going into the lead before two late United goals won the match 4-3,for the second week running Tommy Taylor scored two goals. Over in Yorkshire, United's reserve side lost their first match of the season, 1-0 at Sheffield Wednesday which brought second place Liverpool level, although they had played a match more.

For the second week running Manchester United scored four goals, this time however the opposition, Aston Villa, also scored four. There is something special about Villa Park and Manchester United. Memories go back to the 6-4 FA Cup tie in 1948, whilst up to date the Ryan Giggs goal in the 1999 treble season, other semi final victories and a, seemingly, unbeatable run against Villa there make it a special place for United fans. Back in 1955, Villa went into a two goal lead after twenty minutes before United hit back to go 4-2 up. Wingers Berry and Pegg were in brilliant form whilst Byrne, Jones and goalkeeper Ray Wood all contributed to United's fine display. Colin Webster was handicapped by an ankle injury whilst Jackie Blanchflower had his stamina sapped by a heavy cold. Villa took advantage of this to score two late goals to take a point, with Ray Wood making a fine save late on off Dave Hickson. That point though took United to third place in the league. Back at Old Trafford the reserves got back onto winning ways with a 5-0 thumping of Huddersfield, whilst it was announced this day that the youth cup side would play away at Preston North End in their defence of the trophy.

The week after brought a hive of activity to Manchester United as England used their Cliff training ground in Salford to play a practice match on the Monday night under the floodlights there (none yet at Old Trafford) the day after United played a practice match against the England 'B' side and then on the Wednesday Matt Busby took his side back up to Scotland to play Clyde under their lights. The United match with England 'B' was played behind closed doors and only over half an hour each way. Mind you, probably a good job for the England selectors as United won 6-0 with a hat trick from Taylor and a couple from goal machine Bobby Charlton. The following night the United team went to play Clyde, with a returning Duncan Edwards a big plus although United lost this match 2-1.

The flu bug was sweeping the country and as Edwards returned Ray Wood went down with it bringing Jack Crompton in from captaining the reserve side. This turned out to be Jack's last first team match for the club, a club he served with real pride, credit and ability. He was able to sign off with winning pay as well with United's 3-0 victory over Huddersfield putting them at the top of the table. The reserve side Jack left behind for the day, drew 2-2 at Blackburn still retaining their lead at the top of the table.

Footballers, like all other walks of life, were still subject to National Service at this time, and the story of Bill Foulkes puts this into perspective when United travelled to South Wales to play Cardiff City. He had to travel from his Army headquarters to Porthcawl where United were staying overnight. He left his Army quarters at 2.30 on the Friday and got to South Wales at 11.15 at night!. Billy, and the rest of the United defence, were on top form as they stood firm after Tommy Taylor put United into the lead. Back at Old Trafford the reserves, playing in front of a 7,500 crowd, saw off Blackpool 4-0 with goals from Whelan (2), Charlton and Scanlon.

The Monday evening saw the FA Youth Cup side attempt to retain their defence of the trophy by playing Preston North End at Deepdale. Bobby Charlton continued his amazing scoring run with a hat trick, which along with two from Alex Dawson completed a 5-2 victory. Along with these two in the forward line were future first team players Kenny Morgans and Mark Pearson. Dawson and Pearson dovetailed perfectly and but for Munich would surely have been the Taylor and Viollet of the future.

November 1955
Both the Manchester United first and second teams were in a fine, settled vein of form as we reached November 1955. The first team had gone on a seven match unbeaten run of five victories and two draws, whilst the second team had only lost one match all season and scored goals for fun, extending this with a 5-0 victory in the carried over Manchester Senior Cup Final against Oldham Athletic where they lifted the trophy, against the Oldham first team.

Tommy Taylor was in fine goal scoring form with seven from the eight matches he had played of United's fifteen, extending his sequence with the United goal in a 1-1 draw with Arsenal at Old Trafford on bonfire night 1955. This kept the side top of the league, although the reserves slipped up in their visit to Burnden Park Bolton, losing 1-0.

The week after I was making my first visit to Burnden Park, the first time I was to watch United play an away fixture at the age of eight and a bit. My father Albert, took me via a local Salford coach firm called Fieldsend's with the relatively short journey of about twelve miles seeming to take about three hours! We parked on the open land behind the railway line end of the ground. As we came round to the big forecourt, large queues were already formed for this match, pay at the door fixture with 38,109 eventually getting inside. The queues were so big it was about five minutes into the match when we got a place by one of the large floodlight pylons. This was the first time I had actually seen floodlights as Old Trafford still had not got there's. We were quickly informed that Taylor had again scored to give United an early lead. Coming from Salford I was also pleased to learn that Eddie Colman a nineteen year old from just around the corner from where I lived in Salford was making his debut in the number four shirt for United. Eddie lived in Archie St which in later years was the street that Granada TV used for the start of Coronation St. He would walk down Trafford Road, over the swing bridge and into Old Trafford just like I did; the only difference was that Eddie was actually playing for the team all the locals adored. Eddie had captained the youth team to the FA Youth cup the season before and had quickly settled into reserve football, so Matt Busby had no hesitation to give him his chance as a replacement for Jeff Whitefoot. A man I got to know very well in later life, Nat Lofthouse, was playing for Bolton and he was keen to prove he was as good a player as Tommy Taylor for the England number nine spot, scoring twice as Bolton came from behind to win the match 3-1. My father and I trudged back to the coach park, searching all over for ours, before getting aboard for what seemed an equally long journey home. At Old Trafford, the reserves had got back to winning ways with a 5-0 thumping of Chesterfield, Bobby Charlton with two more goals from the number nine position, scoring against Gordon Banks in the Chesterfield goal, a man he would play alongside eleven years later as England won the World Cup.

After their first defeat in nine matches, Manchester United got back to winning ways with a 3-0 victory over champions Chelsea at Old Trafford. Two more from the prolific Tommy Taylor and one from Roger Bryne emphasised how far these two sides had travelled since the previous April's last match of the season. Chelsea went away from Old Trafford that day as champions with United in fifth place. After this match, United were equal top with Blackpool whilst Chelsea were in fifteenth place. The reserves held their nerve as they drew 2-2 at Liverpool, their closest challenger at the top of the Central League.

It was another top of the table match the Saturday after with United's first team playing away at equal top Blackpool. With Billy Foulkes having to play in an Army Cup tie, United were forced to bring reserve right back Ian Greaves into their side. He stuck well to the task of marking Blackpool left winger Bill Perry, and with Roger Byrne doing his usual excellent marking of Stanley Matthews, United were able to hold the free scoring Blackpool side to a 0-0 draw and preserve top place. With Bobby Charlton scoring the only goal for the reserves to beat Stoke City at Old Trafford, both Manchester United sides were top of the table as we moved into December.

December 1955

That Army Cup tie did not prove costly for Billy Foulkes as Matt Busby brought him back for the visit of fellow championship chasers Sunderland. Goals from Doherty and Viollet won a tightly contested match 2-1 to keep United top, and a single goal at Villa Park did likewise for the reserves.

United had defeat snatched out of victory when they travelled to play Portsmouth. Having been 2-1 up late in the match thanks to Tommy Taylor and David Pegg, Portsmouth then scored twice in the last five minute to steal the points and drop United to second in the table. Travel was not the greatest in the mid fifties and the United side had to travel from Portsmouth to London staying overnight Saturday before coming back on the Sunday. The 'United Review' reported that Sandy Busby, Matt's son, had visited the team in their hotel, Sandy was then playing for the famous amateur side Old Kingstonians. The news came through from Old Trafford that the reserves had beaten Wolves 4-0, with Charlton getting yet another couple of goals.

Bobby Charlton had by this stage of the season scored twenty goals in nineteen games for the reserves, and he was quickly on the goal sheet as the youth side took an early lead against Sunderland in the FA Youth Cup tie at Old Trafford. The Alex Dawson/Mark Pearson link up was also proving fruitful for the young United side and Alex had another two goals as United totally outclassed Sunderland 4-0 to sail on in this competition, still unbeaten in its fourth season.

As Manchester United reached the halfway stage of the season, all their five sides were well in line for winning their respective championships. Both the first and second teams recorded 2-1 victories against Birmingham City and Derby County respectively, with Mark Jones getting a rare winning goal and Ray Wood making a fantastic save from a penalty to preserve United's lead against Birmingham with Charlton and Scanlon getting the goals for the reserves at Derby.

Christmas 1955 saw United playing four games inside a week. On Saturday the 24th they travelled to West Bromwich Albion, played Charlton Athletic at Old Trafford on Boxing Day and travelled to London with the Charlton side to play on the Tuesday, on the Saturday they played Manchester City at Old Trafford. The team turned in a magnificent display at West Brom winning 4-1 with Dennis Viollet scoring a hat trick and Tommy Taylor the other goal. The whole side slotted together so well that many present were reminded of the brilliant 1948 FA Cup winning team. Even though there had been memorable matches with such as Sunderland and Wolverhampton Wanderers at Old Trafford the press opinion was that the display at The Hawthorns was United's best of the season. Indeed, the West Brom Chairman was quoted in saying that United had such good players they could leave the first team there and play the reserves such was the overall strength of the squad. Charlton and Scanlon again were on the score sheet as the reserves beat Newcastle 2-0 at Old Trafford.

One of my Christmas presents was a trip to Old Trafford for the Boxing Day match with Charlton Athletic. My father and I stood in the Old Trafford groundside, level with the scoreboard penalty area. This gave me a good view of the famous Charlton goalkeeper Sam Bartram, who could not have complained if he had been beaten more than the five times he was. John Doherty, Tommy Taylor, two from Dennis Viollet and a Roger Byrne penalty gave United a real championship feeling. The two sides travelled together down to London by train after the match, with the day after, the pouring rain stopping the United flow and totally reversing the roles with Charlton winning 3-0, the first time United had not scored in six matches. That was not the problem for the reserves who hit Bury for six at Gigg Lane then seven the day after with Bobby Charlton scoring a hat trick. Charlton in those times was playing as the out and out centre forward, shooting at every opportunity and gaining lots of goals for his efforts. All this set up for the last fixture of 1955, a Manchester 'derby' with City for both first and second teams.

City had won the previous four matches with United, they had also reached the FA Cup Final the previous season and following on from that success they had a fine side. Bert Trautmann in goal, a classy half back in Ken Barnes, a fearsome left half and captain in Roy Paul, and an all round forward line which included Bobby Johnstone a player Matt Busby had coveted when he was at Hibernian. At last the United fans in the 60,956 crowd, the largest since the war at Old Trafford with thousands locked out, had something to cheer as Tommy Taylor and John Doherty got the second half goals, goals which edged the match 2-1 and put the side clear at the top as 1956 beckoned. The reserves won over at Maine Road 3-0, which made it eight wins on the trot with a goal total of 26 for and 3 against.

As the New Year loomed, 1956 offered a chance for Matt Busby's faith in his young players to fulfil their undoubted talent, he had a relatively settled side in; WOOD, FOULKES, BYRNE, COLMAN, JONES, EDWARDS, BERRY, DOHERTY, TAYLOR, VIOLLET and PEGG giving an average age of 22.

Chapter SIX
A Champions Diary, Part Two

January 1956

The first offering of 1956 was a visit to Second Division Bristol Rovers for a tricky FA Cup tie. As mentioned earlier, in the mid 1950's there was no Match of the Day, no Talksport, no Mobiles (not many land lines either!) so Radio and Newspapers were the only way of keeping in contact with sporting matters. Manchester had two Evening Newspapers, Manchester Evening News and Evening Chronicle, and they both had Saturday sports editions, The Pink and The Green. It was sometimes these papers which gave first information of an away match although Sports Report at 5pm on the Radio was another place to get those elusive results. The news that came through to Manchester from Bristol on Saturday 7th January 1956 did not make good reading or listening to as the top of the First Division, Manchester United, had been totally outplayed by a mid table Second Division side, Bristol Rovers losing 4-0 before a full house of 35,872.Whilst United were without Duncan Edwards and both Berry and Colman arrived late at the teams hotel due to family illness and National Service respectively, it was still a major cup shock.

If you had gone to Old Trafford that day to see the reserves play Everton, you had an aborted afternoon. Severe fog around the ground caused an abandonment of the match fifteen minutes in with the game scoreless. On other afternoons though, this was also a way of keeping up with the first team action as the score was given on the scoreboard situated behind the goal at the Manchester end of the ground. Every fifteen minutes the scoreboard attendant would open letter A and put in the score. Regarding the fog, this was not uncommon in these days. You had the air swirling from the canal, the smoke bellowing out of the Trafford Park factory chimneys, and then the steam engines bellowing out as they passed the main stand side of the Old Trafford ground. The fog this day was what they called a real 'Pea Souper!'

A chance to put the Cup debacle out of the system came the following Saturday when Sheffield United visited Old Trafford. Goals from Berry, Pegg and Taylor duly delivered the points with a 3-1 victory. Billy Whelan was given another chance at inside right in place of John Doherty and, indeed, the 'United Review' for this Sheffield match is the first time that the long regarded first eleven for the team known as the 'Busby Babes' was recorded, this was; WOOD, FOULKES, BYRNE, COLMAN, JONES, EDWARDS, BERRY, WHELAN, TAYLOR VIOLLET and PEGG. It was made up of two nineteen year olds in Edwards and Colman, two twenty year olds Whelan and Pegg, two twenty two year olds Foulkes and Jones, a twenty three year old in Wood, two twenty four year olds in Taylor and Viollet, Roger Byrne at twenty six and Johnny Berry being the 'old' man at twenty nine. Over in Sheffield, the reserves won 4-0 to lead the Central League by four points with two games in hand.

Billy Whelan justified his promotion at Preston the week after by scoring United's goal, unfortunately Preston scored three! Tommy Taylor missed this match due to an injury with Colin Webster stepping in. Whilst the mood was down after this set back, that feeling would not be felt again as the team went unbeaten for the rest of the season. Preston reserves did halt the runaway Manchester United reserves at Old Trafford by holding them to a 0-0 draw, the first time they had been held in nine games and already having scored eighty four goals to their name after twenty eight matches.

On Saturday 28th January 1956, Manchester United's FA Youth Cup side was allowed to play their 4th round tie at Old Trafford in the afternoon against Newcastle United. This was the date for the 4th round of the FA Cup so with the first team knocked out an even younger version of Matt Busby's 'Babes' attracted a massive crowd of 26,282 to see what they were all about. The crowd was not disappointed! The renowned reporter, Alf Clarke of the Manchester Evening Chronicle who had reported in the 'United Review' since its inception in the early 1930's was fulsome in his praise for the side."It is difficult to imagine that the standard of football being served up could be done so by lads so young. I have seldom seen such brilliance from teenagers."One of the travelling Newcastle United Directors accompanying their side said to Clarke, "This is a great side, but how did we let Bobby Charlton slip through our fingers, for we had been watching him since he was eleven year old" Bobby, of course came from Ashington close to Newcastle and it was, indeed, St James Park that Bobby and his elder brother Jack Charlton watched their first football matches. The time that Joe Armstrong put in on behalf of Manchester United scouting the stars of the future could not be undervalued. Bobby certainly turned the style on in this match scoring two goals as United ran out 7-1 victors. On the same day Manchester United's first team went over the Pennines to play Second Division Leeds United in a friendly as they had both been knocked out of the FA Cup. This time United had no problem with Second Division opposition and won 4-1 with a near full strength side.

February 1956
There was a strong feeling now around Old Trafford that if they got over the fixture list for February still at the top of the table the return of the League Championship to Old Trafford would be a real possibility. The first test was a visit from Lancashire rivals Burnley.

Billy Foulkes, Duncan Edwards and Eddie Colman were still serving in the forces, but it was Billy who suffered by losing his place with Ian Greaves again replacing him, and staying in the side for the rest of the season. Burnley was a strong side themselves, third at the start of this match five points behind United but a game in hand. They had an inside forward I always liked watching, the Northern Ireland International Jimmy McIlroy. It took all of Duncan Edwards's skill to nullify McIlroy which allowed Taylor and Viollet to score the two goals for a very important United victory. The reserves went over to Turf Moor to play Burnley, and having been stopped from scoring in their last fixture with Preston, they again were scoreless, only this time Burnley put three in their net to inflict a shock defeat.

A trip to Kenilworth Road to play Luton Town was made more difficult by the British Army! They had arranged a match with the Belgian Army in Brussels and called up Billy Foulkes, Eddie Colman and Duncan Edwards with Ian Greaves, Freddie Goodwin and Jackie Blanchflower stepping up to the first team. A second consecutive 2-0 victory returned the points to Old Trafford thanks to goals from Billy Whelan and Dennis Viollet. Showing the real strength of Matt Busby's squad, the reserves, despite losing three regular players, achieved a 3-1 victory over Leeds United to stay two points clear.

Wolverhampton Wanderers away was always going to be a defining test as to whether real championship hopes would be fulfilled. Although Matt Busby was able to call on his three Army players, only two of them, Colman and Edwards, returned straight to the side. Busby felt the time was right to give Ian Greaves an extended run and, in fact, he stayed at right back for the rest of the season. Greaves was going to be really tested at Molineux, but along with Mark Jones and Roger Byrne the United defence was in magnificent form allowing Tommy Taylor to score two goals and give United a third consecutive victory by the same score. Jones, and goalkeeper Ray Wood, had celebrations off the pitch as well as both became fathers to make it a really feel good atmosphere around Old Trafford. With thirty one fixtures of the forty two game season gone, Manchester United were six points clear of Blackpool, although the Seasiders had a match in hand. To complete the good news, despite being held to a 1-1 draw at Old Trafford by Sheffield Wednesday, the reserves stayed two points clear of Liverpool, both having played thirty matches.

The reserves had another 1-1 draw, this time away to Huddersfield Town as we reached the end of February 1956, with a Billy Whelan goal giving United victory over Aston Villa at Old Trafford. This ended a testing month with four victories, seven goals for and none against as the title seemed set for Manchester United, and the start of a new dynasty for Matt Busby, particularly with the rest of his club's teams all in dominant form in their respective leagues and a youth side which was well on its way to retaining the FA Youth Cup for the fourth successive season.

March 1956
Manchester United's last visit to Stamford Bridge to play Chelsea had seen an unforgettable match which United won 6-5 against the side that would win the championship of 1955. Over 60,000 turned up for that match, as we moved into March 1956 with Chelsea below halfway, there was a crowd of 32,000 to see the heir apparent, Manchester United. Tommy Taylor scored his twentieth goal of the season as United again won a high scoring match, this time 4-2. Dennis Viollet scored twice and David Pegg got in the act as United wooed the London fans with their exciting brand of football. At Old Trafford the reserves after constant attacking the Blackburn Rovers goal

found themselves 0-2 down. News from Chelsea via the scoreboard information every fifteen minutes, seemed to lift the team and the crowd of over 7,000, as they scored five times to stay top of the table, Charlton with two of the goals.

The cover of the 'United Review' for the visit of Cardiff City was covered with the news that a Testimonial match would be played at the end of the season for John Aston. He was a true Manchester United player, developed through the youth teams, winner of an FA Cup and League Championship medal and an England International. Whether it was as a full back or in the forward positions, John did what was best for the club. John had suffered badly with ill health, spending long periods in hospital and the club responded by allowing the Manchester United fans to show their appreciation at the end of the season. Twelve years on, his son also called John, would be Man of the Match in the European Cup Final for his father's side. Back in 1956, and Cardiff stopped the runaway leaders by earning a 1-1 draw at Old Trafford with Roger Byrne scoring for United in front of an appreciative crowd of 44,693.The reserves enjoyed a day out at the seaside by beating Blackpool 2-1.

The previous season United had played a double header of youth team in the morning and reserves in the afternoon. In March 1956 this was reversed with the reserves playing Bolton at 11am on the Saturday morning and the youths playing Bexley Heath & Welling in the afternoon. The reserves side won 2-0 with goals from Doherty and Blanchflower with Bobby Charlton needed for the youth match. That drew a crowd of over 22,000 with Charlton showing his amazing goal scoring form by scoring five goals in an overwhelming 11-1 victory over the South London side that had links with Charlton Athletic, earning a two legged semi final with Bolton Wanderers. On the same day, the United first team had attracted a crowd of over 50,000 to Highbury as London were convinced they were seeing the top side in England. Dennis Viollet scored again and why he was not attracting the eye of England manager Walter Winterbottom, who was present at Highbury, alongside his partner in crime Tommy Taylor one could only wonder. Viollet's goal earned United a point from a 1-1 draw although Roger Byrne had the chance to secure both points but blazed a penalty over the Arsenal bar.

Bolton Wanderers came to Old Trafford looking to secure a double over the probable champions on the Saturday before Easter as United strove to get those points to secure the title. An Australian cricketer Ken Grieves, who also played for the 'other' Old Trafford side, Lancashire County Cricket Club, was in goal for Bolton and he did his very best to keep a clean sheet. Thankfully, Tommy Taylor scored the only goal which kept United's lead over Blackpool to five points, although they did have a game in hand over United. When the reserves suffered a surprise 1-0 defeat at Chesterfield it meant the forthcoming Easter break would be a defining period for the destination of the first and second team's title aspirations.

Easter 1956 saw the usual three matches played in four days. Good Friday brought Newcastle United to Old Trafford and a bumper crowd of 58,994 were there to try and help Matt Busby's young side over the line. An emphatic 5-2 victory was the perfect start with goals from Viollet (2), Taylor, Pegg and a goal from the returning John Doherty. He had not featured since the heavy defeat at Bristol Rovers in the FA Cup back in January which had opened the door for Billy Whelan, but an ankle injury to Billy gave Doherty the chance to get back in the side and he took it brilliantly with a marvellous goal. This emphasised the quality Matt Busby had in depth, shown by the fact that when Foulkes dropped out for Army duties Ian Greaves had stepped in and could not be dropped. Eddie Colman had done the same with his chance when Jeff Whitefoot was left out in November. Of course, this was helped by a reserve side that had automatic replacements in every position and they kept their pursuit of the reserve title up with a merited 0-0 draw at West Bromwich Albion.

Twenty Four hours later the reserves lit up Old Trafford with a tremendous display to blow away their nearest rivals Liverpool, winning 4-0. This really put them in the driving seat, and the first team continued their fine form with a Tommy Taylor double defeating Huddersfield Town at Leeds Road. One more Easter fixture then it would be the defining Blackpool fixture at Old Trafford...

April 1956

Easter Monday at Old Trafford saw the reserves turn in a magnificent display to totally outplay West Bromwich Albion by 8-0.Six of those goals were scored by young eighteen year old Bobby Charlton, making it thirty seven for the season at that time. With Liverpool reserves losing their match this left the title on a plate for United. Across in Charlton's homeland, the North East, United's first team were being held 0-0 by Newcastle United, although a victory, due to points dropped by Blackpool, would have given the title to United. That pleasure would have to now wait until the following Saturday when Blackpool, the only realistic challenger, were in town to face United.

That match is recorded in the first chapter of this book, the 2-1 victory bringing the title back to Old Trafford for the first time in four years, Matt Busby's second title to go alongside the FA Cup he guided the side to in 1948. Three major trophies in the ten years since the war was a fair reflection of the type of football Busby was bringing to the club. This time he also had such a conveyor belt running through the club that the success looked to be on tap for years to come.

Manchester United embarked on a spell of friendly matches in the month of April. Two visits to Scotland to play Dundee and Glasgow Celtic, plus a trip to Southern Ireland to play Home Farm. The Dundee match came forty eight hours after the United side had celebrated long into the Saturday night the success of winning the championship and with no Bryne, Colman, Edwards, Whelan or Taylor the side were hammered 5-1 by the Scottish side. There was also a major injury scare for goalkeeper Ray Wood who was carried off, thankfully with a sore leg as opposed to the feared broken one.

The week after the championship clinching victory over Blackpool at Old Trafford, the reserves deservedly won the Central League title even though they were held to a goalless draw by Aston Villa. This was some feat by Villa as the reserves had scored well over a hundred goals with still two matches to play. For the second Saturday running Matt Busby missed seeing his first team in action. With the league title in the bag, he went to Hampden Park to support Roger Byrne, Duncan Edwards and Tommy Taylor as they played for England against Scotland. This called for wholesale changes in the United side that played Sunderland at Roker Park with Bent, McGuinness and Blanchflower stepping in. Wilf McGuinness actually scored his first goal for United in this match with another from Whelan earning the new champions a 2-2 draw.

Following the Sunderland match the team travelled over to stay in Troon prior to a charity match against Celtic in Glasgow. A much stronger United side showed Scotland a better side of their play than at Dundee the week before and played out a 2-2 draw. This was on the Monday evening; forty eight hours after, the youth team played their first leg semi final tie against Bolton Wanderers at Old Trafford and a crowd over 20,000 witnessed a very hard match with Bolton knocking United off their stride which along with an outstanding display by their goalkeeper Joe Dean earned them a 1-1 draw giving them thoughts of knocking the holders out of the competition they had won for its first three seasons.

Having played before the largest Old Trafford crowd since the war in their previous match against Blackpool, it was somewhat surprising that less than 40,000 were present to see Roger Bryne lift the league championship when Portsmouth ended the season on 21st April 1956. I was one of those there and can still remember being in the United Road side of the ground to see Byrne go up one side of the players tunnel receive the trophy and come down the other to show to the crowd. Dennis Viollet scored the only goal for the match to leave United high and dry at the top of the table, the Busby Babes winning the first of what would be, hopefully, many, many trophies.

Two different types of friendly matches then took place within the following week. United flew to Dublin to play John Carey's old side Home Farm and treated the 23,000 Dubliners to a fine display winning 4-0. The team then returned to play an All Star XI in a testimonial match for former player Johnny Aston. The crowd size of 40,350 was two thousand more than had seen the league championship lifted the week before, a fitting response to one of Manchester United's loyalist players whose career had been cut short by illness. United won a hard fought match, no end of season kick about this, by 2-1. Mind you it is worth noting that old and present stars such as Frank Swift, John Carey, Henry Cockburn, Stan Pearson, Jack Rowley, Johnny Morris, Tom Finney, Tommy Docherty and Nat Lofthouse turned out to show their respect to a great player.

With the season over and both first and second teams having won their respective championships, it was left to the youth side to see if they could make it a club hat trick. Their visit to Burnden Park drew a crowd of over 24,000 with the closeness of the first leg blown away as United won comfortably 3-0. This brought Chesterfield to Old Trafford for the first leg of the FA Youth Cup final. Chesterfield's senior side played in the old

Third Division North so this was an excellent effort by the club's youngsters. When after half an hour United had eased into a 3-0 lead including yet another Bobby Charlton goal, it seemed all over and done with. In the end, Chesterfield gave Manchester United their closest scare in the competition to date by pulling two second half goals back and going one nil up in the tie at their home ground. Over 24,000 had attended the Old Trafford tie and the Recreation ground Chesterfield was full to its limits with over 15,000 sensing a real upset, all aware that their young goalkeeper Gordon Banks was a true star in the making. It took a 90th minute equaliser on the night by outside left Dennis Fidler to give United a draw and the cup on a 4-3 aggregate. A very relived and proud Wilf McGuinness lifted the trophy for United, their fourth year of winning this prestigious trophy.

Manchester United played forty three first team fixtures in league and FA Cup in 1955/56 although they did play a number of friendlies. They had true cover in all positions but only used sixteen players for over ten or more matches. Centre Half Mark Jones actually played in all forty three matches, with Edwards Taylor, Berry, Viollet, Pegg, Wood and Byrne playing over thirty games. Tommy Taylor was leading scorer with twenty five goals from his thirty four matches.

As in the last season the club visited Scandinavia for a post season tour winning all four fixtures in Sweden and Denmark, a prelude to playing competitive matches in Europe as Manchester United decided that they would compete in the second season of the new European Cup. 1956/57 promised to be one of the most exciting in the club's fine history...

Chapter SEVEN
Europe beckons for The Busby Babes

Manchester United moved into totally new territory in 1956. Not just the League Championship (defending as the champions) a tilt at the FA Cup, but also new horizons in Europe. The European Cup. Mind you, but for Matt Busby it would not have happened. The Football authorities had told Chelsea the year before not to compete, Busby and The Manchester United board, were of sterner stuff. They felt that this new competition for the champions of nations was a real step forward, particularly after a devastating World War only ten years or so before. Let us continue a weekly diary of how events panned out.

August 1956
Life is full of fate, where you were, why you missed out etc. For Ian Greaves, the pre season training which resulted in him getting injured meant he missed taking up his place in the Manchester United championship side as they attempted to defend their hard won title. This meant another chance for Bill Foulkes to re-establish himself as the Manchester United right back. Bill never looked back...

Bill was still in the forces along with Eddie Colman and Duncan Edwards, to be joined at the start of the season by Bobby Charlton. The first three took their places in the Manchester United line up for the season's opener against Birmingham City at Old Trafford. Although it was mid August the weather was not of a cricket variety as torrential rain, falling on an already sodden turf, made the conditions farcical with the ball unable to flow, indeed, the match must have been close to being abandoned at various stages. The 32,752 were able to see the full ninety minutes though with two goals from Dennis Viollet earning United a 2-2 draw with Mark Jones getting on the score sheet for Birmingham. The 'United Review' carried a new innovation this season, a Token Sheet. This proved great foresight by the club as they were to be involved in a record breaking amount of fixtures, culminating in major matches for the club. With Foulkes back in the line up the United side for the start of the season was; WOOD, FOULKES, BYRNE, COLMAN, JONES, EDWARDS, BERRY, WHELAN, TAYLOR, VIOLLET and PEGG. The Central League side, also as defending champions, had a disappointing start, losing 3-2 at Derby County.

The season was further underway with a visit to Deepdale to play Preston North End forty eight hours later. Following the heavy rain, bright sunshine greeted the sides with United getting into a winning run by taking the points 3-2 thanks to two late goals by Billy Whelan and Dennis Viollet, Tommy Taylor getting the other. Whelan, incidentally, had won his first International cap for Eire in the summer. Back at Old Trafford, the reserves also welcomed the sun by hammering Preston 6-0.

As August came to an end, it was again the weather which was a big talking point as glorious sunshine at The Hawthorns welcomed the West Bromwich Albion and United sides, being replaced by a thunderstorm in the second half! The inside forward trio of Whelan, Taylor and Viollet had started the season in great form, a late header from Whelan complementing the first half goals from the other two to give United all the points in a 3-2 victory. The reserves took a quick liking to their Old Trafford surroundings by scoring another six, this time against Chesterfield who managed two themselves. Albert Scanlon had started the season really well with five of the fourteen goals the reserves had scored. The reserves scored another three at Preston on the Monday night before the two senior sides met at Old Trafford on the Wednesday.

Dennis Viollet was a very under rated player. His goal scoring feats for Manchester United bare standing with any of the clubs' great strikers, and indeed, in later years he scored more league goals in a season than any other player for the club, before or since. When Preston visited Old Trafford for a quick return fixture, it was Dennis who put United in front, and then got a late winner as the scores were tied at 2-2. He also got the other goal so a hat trick in match four gave him a return of seven goals from those first four games, and all five goals United had scored at Old Trafford so far.

September 1956

The big news the first day of September was about matters OFF the field of play as Portsmouth visited Old Trafford. The club programme the 'United Review' informed on its cover of the new floodlights which were about to transform Old Trafford. Work had just commenced for the installation of four pylons, each 160 feet high, holding 54 floodlights, equal to millions of candlepower. More clubs were looking into this new initiative, Maine Road across the city had, of course, already got their lights which opened up all sorts of games that could attract more supporters at a night as opposed to say 2.30 on a Wednesday afternoon. The cost was expected to be £40,000 and, hopefully, would be ready for use towards the end of the season. There was also news that the return leg of the forthcoming European Cup tie with Anderlecht would be held at Maine Road with a night kick off under City's lights, as opposed to the original idea of playing on a Wednesday afternoon at Old Trafford. On the pitch United easily beat Portsmouth 3-0 with Berry, Pegg and Viollet getting the goals. Although the side had an average age of 23, only Colman (31 games) and Whelan (25 games) had played less than 70 matches and this game was for example Duncan Edwards 100th appearance for United and he was still only nineteen. United reserves travelled over to West Bromwich and came back with a 2-2 draw.

Manchester United embarked on a series of three away matches in September, league matches at Chelsea and Newcastle United, and the first ever English tie in the European Cup at Anderlecht, champions of Belgium in Brussels. Stamford Bridge was becoming a happy home for United and goals from Taylor and Whelan secured a fine 2-1 away victory. Fans of other clubs were flocking to see Manchester United when they were in town and over 50,000 packed St James Park Newcastle see the local heroes at least stop this winning run of United by taking a point in a 1-1 draw. Still, 5 victories and two draws, along with being unchanged, was a great return from the first seven matches of the season. Over at Old Trafford the reserves beat Newcastle 3-1 to give them four victories a draw and one defeat from their first six fixtures.

That became two defeats on the Monday evening as the reserves went down 3-1 at Huddersfield, although some of the players were making the trip to Brussels for the European Cup tie which weakened the side. Lower down the United line ups at this time saw players such as Morgans, Brennan, Dawson, Pearson playing in the 'A' side with a very young John Giles playing for the Junior team at inside left.

The great European adventure for Manchester United began on Wednesday September 12th in the Belgian capital Brussels. Sadly, United had to make their first change of the season on their eighth match with Jackie Blanchflower taking over from Duncan Edwards at left half. A full house in the Park Astrid stadium of 35,000 saw United march on with goals from Dennis Viollet and Tommy Taylor giving what looked a comfortable victory. Anderlecht though, missed a penalty at a crucial period in the match and then came Taylor's goal with a quite brilliant header, emphasising the quality he had as a centre forward.

An Old Trafford crowd of 48,078 welcomed back the European heroes with Edwards back in the side; they easily beat Sheffield Wednesday 4-1. Almost the complete forward line of Berry, Whelan, Taylor and Viollet scored the goals, just leaving David Pegg off the score sheet. This left United top of the table after eight games a point clear of Leeds United. The reserves were seventh in their table, another 3-1 defeat, this time at Sheffield Wednesday not helping matters.

The visit of local rivals Manchester City the week after produced an even bigger crowd, this time 53,525 inside Old Trafford for the meeting of the previous seasons Champions and FA Cup winners. Dennis Viollet, a Manchester lad himself, scored another goal his tenth in ten first team matches including the European tie. His link with Taylor, who also scored, was almost telepathic, although in fairness, the whole side was linking brilliantly as a 2-0 victory kept United clear at the top and fully prepared for the home leg of the European Cup against Anderlecht the following Wednesday. The reserves came back from Maine Road with a 1-1 draw thanks to a late equaliser from Albert Scanlon, his seventh goal in nine appearances.

Whilst sides from overseas had played at Old Trafford in the past, most notably and poignantly Red Star Belgrade in the Festival of Britain match of 1951, it was mainly the stars from across the border in Scotland which gave a more regular feeling of 'foreign' football to Mancunians. This was to change forever on Wednesday 26th September 1956 when Anderlecht came to play the second leg tie, not at Old Trafford but across the city at Maine Road due to floodlighting issues. Whilst it was not deemed an all ticket match, there were reserved seats to be bought for the main stand at 7/6 (38p) and 5/6 (28p). I still remember the night of September 26th well even though I was not at the game. The Manchester Evening papers, Chronicle and News, brought the excitement of European football alive to a young nine year old Salford boy. Inside the back page they showed pictures and gave information on these Anderlecht players who had travelled from what seemed a faraway place to rainy Manchester. Some of those names which intrigued me were; FELIX WEEK (Goalkeeper) 'Regarded as one of the best keepers on the continent' JOSEPH JURION (inside forward) ' youngest of the Anderlecht side at nineteen, but a real danger man in attack. Regarded as the Stanley Matthews of Belgian soccer, already a full International' JOSEPH MERMANS (inside forward) 'Aged thirty Four, the captain of Anderlecht and idol of Belgian football. Can play anywhere in attack, fifty seven caps and appeared for the Rest of Europe as well'.

Wow! They all seemed like supermen and my team had gone to their ground and won 2-0. This time United were to go barmy and beat this team of superstars 10-0, yes 10-0! In one of Manchester United's greatest ever performances, Dennis Viollet scored four, Tommy Taylor three, Billy Whelan two and Johnny Berry one. The whole side then desperately tried to get outside left Pegg onto the score sheet, particularly as he had played a brilliant game. The Busby Babes were on the march in England and Europe now...

After ten league matches without a change, Matt Busby had to introduce a new centre half due to a thigh strain to Mark Jones. Into the side came twenty one year old Ronnie Cope, the former England schoolboy international, his first opportunity to play at senior level. With a big London crowd of over 62,000 trying to encourage them, Arsenal were rocked as United went into a two goal lead thanks to Berry and an absolute gem from Billy Whelan. Arsenal did respond in the second half and, thanks to a disputed penalty, made it a rousing finish but United held onto a 2-1 victory and go two points clear at the top of the table. Normally Jackie Blanchflower would have been entrusted as Jones replacement but Manchester United reserves had a very special match at Old Trafford as defending Champions against The Rest and Jackie took his place as centre half. United fielded a reasonably strong side but despite taking the lead from Alex Dawson, The Rest blew them away and scored seven goals without further reply!

October 1956

It cannot be stated enough how footballers, and football clubs, were stretched in the mid 1950's. Not only was there the advent of the 'new' European Cup to fit into the playing schedules but players were called up to play for their forces side as well, whilst International calls were still played on a Saturday at times. So, in between the fixture at Highbury against Arsenal and the visit of another London side Charlton Athletic to Old Trafford, Billy Whelan played for Eire against Denmark whilst Eddie Colman and reserve goalkeeper Gordon Clayton appeared for The Army against Everton at Goodison Park. Bobby Charlton would also have appeared in that fixture but he had been injured playing for United reserves at Maine Road a couple of weeks earlier.

The fixture with his namesake club however, was to give Bobby Charlton, later to become one of the greatest players in the clubs history, his league debut. This came about due to the Ireland versus England International being played at Belfast's Windsor Park on the same day. Roger Byrne, Duncan Edwards and Tommy Taylor were picked for England with Ireland picking Jackie Blanchflower. Geoff Bent and Wilf McGuinness also came into the team, whilst Jones returned from his injury. How Bobby Charlton responded to his chance! Playing centre forward as replacement for Tommy Taylor, his two excellent goals in the first half helped give United a 4-2 victory, with Bent and McGuinness again proving how good they were as potential first team players. I was at this match, stood in the main stand side paddock in a crowd of 41,439 all of us unaware we was witness to the start of one of football's greatest future players. Interesting point about Charlton Athletic at this time, they had five South African players in their squad a couple of whom also played cricket for Kent. The reserves continued a disappointing spell by losing 1-0 at Blackburn.

Forty eight hours after one of the stars of recent FA Youth cup sides for Manchester United had made his full debut, the next batch of young stars were on show at The Cliff under the training grounds floodlights before a crowd of 3,000 playing Burnley at the start of this seasons campaign. One name was on everyone's lips after the match, Alex Dawson. Already a reserve player, Alex scored all five goals as they went through to the next round 5-2.

He was back in the reserve side the following Saturday when Blackpool visited Old Trafford. Playing in a very good looking forward line of Morgans, Doherty, Charlton, Dawson and Scanlon, none of them could manage a goal whilst Blackpool did score one to earn a surprise victory. The first team had another trip to the North East, drawing a 50,000 crowd, this time at Sunderland. A full strength United side continued their unbeaten run with a 3-1 victory, Viollet, Whelan and an own goal securing the points. A second half display of power and skill totally dominated the home side as United stayed firmly at the top of the table.

European competition was now regularly on the mid week agenda and it certainly had wetted the Manchester football appetite. A massive 75,598 packed out Maine Road for the visit of German champions Dortmund Borussia. Busby's Babes were like a well oiled machine now and inside thirty five minutes they were 3-0 up. Dennis Viollet who was a goal machine this season, scored twice and David Pegg a third to have the German side fearing another Anderlecht type mauling. Somehow they rode the storm and by the middle of the second half started to cause problems themselves. Two goals were pulled back making the final score of 3-2 a tricky proposition for United, although away goals did not count at this time. The referee incidentally became a world famous official, Leo Horn.

Returning to their own 'home' of Old Trafford, United fans amongst the 43,151 crowd myself included, confidently expected to give lowly Everton a good hiding. Bobby Charlton took his place for his second United appearance in place of Dennis Viollet who still had a niggling injury. Bobby scored again, but Everton scored five! Shattering

United's long standing unbeaten twenty six match run. Another man who had played in both of Bobby Charlton's appearances, but for the opposition was an inside forward called Jimmy Gauld. He had played for Charlton Athletic, and then was transferred to Everton in the mean time. Gauld became infamous in the early 1960's as the man heavily involved in the betting scandal which rocked football. It has to be said that people just could not believe this Everton result, not only were they playing poorly all season and United top of the league and unbeaten but Everton introduced a debutant in goal Albert Dunlop. He had a brilliant match, but even so it was one of football's shock results. Jimmy Murphy was not at a United game this Saturday as he had been invited to manage the Wales side against Scotland at Cardiff. He would have been shocked at the Old Trafford result but happier that his reserves had managed to end their poor run beating Everton 3-2 at Goodison Park.

Manchester had become the hot bed of football in the previous season, United winning the League title and City the FA Cup. This meant that the two sides would contest the Charity Shield which was switched to Maine Road so it could be played under floodlights and also televised live on the BBC. This probably affected the crowd size to 30,495, a cool 45,000 less than had seen United play on the same pitch the week before against Dortmund. Whilst United won the Shield thanks to yet another goal from the returning Dennis Viollet it was the injury to their goalkeeper Ray Wood which made all the headlines. Ray hurt his thigh and had to go off with Duncan Edwards putting the green jersey on for a short time. What the crowd, and indeed the BBC commentator, did not notice was that it was not Wood who returned to goal but young David Gaskell who had only joined United from school in the summer and had been playing for the youth sides. He played really well keeping City at bay helping United's victory.

On the Saturday he was in the reserve side at Old Trafford against Leeds helping them to a 4-1 victory, a side that had everyone in it, including sixteen year old Gaskell, who had played for the first team. The reserve side that day was; GASKELL, GREAVES, BENT, GOODWIN, BLANCHFLOWER, McGUINNESS, WEBSTER, DOHERTY, DAWSON, CHARLTON and SCANLON. A team which would have given many a first division side a game. It was still the goalkeeping position which was making the news for the first team on the same day. Ray Wood still felt his thigh problem and it meant eighteen year old Tony Hawksworth, who had only played a couple of reserve games before, being promoted for his debut in a top of the table match at Blackpool before 33,000 people. Like Gaskell he made a good impression and although letting two goals in he was part of a team that came away with a 2-2 draw thanks to a late Tommy Taylor header, his second goal of the game.

Chapter EIGHT

A Busy Schedule

November 1956

The Manchester public responded to the meeting of the young Busby Babes and the hardened Wolverhampton Wanderers with just short of 60,000 witnessing a marvellous display from United. A 3-0 victory with goals from Whelan, Taylor and Pegg showed how the pendulum had now swung firmly to Old Trafford. Confirmation was given in the 'United Review' that Jack Crompton had left United to join Luton Town as coach, Jack was a marvellous, loyal player for Manchester United and it was significant that United could call on his replacement Ray Wood to return from injury in this important match. Although the reserves had a set back over at Bolton losing an excellent match 3-2, Alex Dawson, still only sixteen, was making a fine goal scoring impression whenever he played, the Bolton reserve goalkeeper Ken Grieves, also the Lancashire Cricketer, could not believe Dawson's young age, likening him to Jack Rowley.

Dawson was again in goal scoring form when the FA Youth Cup side travelled to Huddersfield in the next round of the competition. Before he found the net though, United were two down, one of the goals scored by a certain Denis Law! This was Matt Busby's first sight of his fellow Scotsman and he was suitably impressed to make Huddersfield an offer which was turned down. Six years later he would become one of the greatest players to appear for Manchester United...

The goals continued to flow for Alex Dawson when he appeared at Old Trafford for the reserves in their match with Aston Villa. This time he scored a hat trick as the reserves got back to winning ways with a 5-2 victory. Sadly for the first team the Bolton hoodoo struck again as the Wanderers beat them 2-0 at Burnden Park, ending an away unbeaten run since the previous January at Preston. This defeat actually knocked United off the top of the table on goal difference to Tottenham Hotspur.

Bobby Charlton had played at Bolton as Dennis Viollet again reported a worrying injury. He kept his place the following week when Leeds United visited Old Trafford, with another Charlton, brother Jack playing at centre half for them. Leeds were actually third on their return to the First Division mainly due to the performance of the magnificent John Charles, who like Duncan Edwards, could play virtually anywhere. They were also managed by Raich Carter, himself a top class former England International. This intriguing fixture drew a crowd of 52,131, sadly not to see Edwards who dropped out with injury, which with the return European Cup tie the following week was a big worry. Two goals from Billy Whelan and one from Bobby Charlton earned a hard fought 3-2 victory with Charles amongst the goals scoring a penalty for the visitors.

A freezing cold Rote Erde Stadium in Dortmund with a full house of 44,570, including many British troops stationed in Germany saw Ray Wood's finest display in his green goalkeeping jersey for Manchester United. Duncan Edwards returned not in his usual number six shirt but the number ten instead of Charlton with McGuinness staying at left half to protect the single goal advantage. Thanks to Wood's heroics a 0-0 draw proved enough to take United through to the quarter finals of this growing competition. Bert Trautmann, the Manchester City goalkeeper, had travelled with United to his native Germany to act as translator.

From Germany it was a trip to high flying Tottenham Hotspur on the Saturday. Spurs had lost to Sheffield Wednesday the previous Saturday when United were beating Leeds so it was a real top of the table fixture at White Hart Lane before a 57,000 crowd. Two goals down inside the first seven minutes and now without the injured Mark Jones as well as Viollet, United proceeded to put on a power display which had a real 'champion' feel about it. Goals from Johnny Berry and Eddie Colman, his first senior goal, kept United two points clear at the top of the table. It was a sign of the improving travel times when it was reported that to return from Germany the previous Thursday it had taken one and half hours to fly back to Manchester, whilst to travel back from London on the Saturday night after the Tottenham match it took five hours and on a train with no heating! Back at Old Trafford the reserves continued their revival with a 2-0 victory over Wolves with Bobby Charlton and John Doherty getting the goals.

December 1956
In Dennis Viollet's continued absence, Edwards stayed at inside left, and scored, as United beat Luton Town 3-1 at Old Trafford. Jack Crompton, in his new role as coach of Luton, made a quick return to Manchester but could only watch as Pegg and Taylor joined Duncan on the score sheet. Interestingly, in the next two weeks United would play consecutive matches in the city of Birmingham, with the 'United Review' showing where the train would leave from in Manchester and to which part of Birmingham they would go. Now, whilst I am a Salford lad, I have a decent knowledge of Manchester but don't remember where Mayfield station was which is where the train to Villa would go from to Witton, the station nearest Villa Park. The week after the train to Birmingham City's nearest station, Bordesley, would go from Manchester London Road. Both trips would cost 10/6 (53p). That United programme also updated the 'A','B' and Junior sides progress, with all being at or next to the top of the table. The juniors had won all eleven matches played with seventy six goals scored; two players who would eventually make their mark from this side were John Giles and Nobby Lawton. The reserves travelled to Barnsley and came back with a 2-2 draw.

Manchester United's journeys to Birmingham begin in fine style with a second consecutive 3-1 victory at Aston Villa. Viollet returned, and scored, along with two from Tommy Taylor, although Roger Byrne dropped out to give Geoff Bent another opportunity. The reserves beat Sheffield United 1-0 at Old Trafford and repeated the score the week after when they played Stoke City in a morning kick off to enable the youth team to play Sunderland in the afternoon FA Youth Cup. Another large crowd watched in admiration as the next batch of United starlets won 3-1, although the score being displayed from the first team's match at Birmingham City did not make good reading as it was updated every fifteen minutes, Birmingham winning 3-1. Billy Whelan scored United's goal and he, Berry, Pegg, Colman and Foulkes had played in every match so far at the half way stage which saw United still at the top of the table.

The weather and petrol rationing caused one or two problems around Christmas time 1956. A combination of fog and West Bromwich Albion being unable to get to Old Trafford due to the over stretched railways because of the petrol situation meant the postponement of the Old Trafford match, and indeed the reserves visit to Chesterfield. It had already been decided to re arrange the Christmas Day fixture at Cardiff City until later in the season because of the petrol situation and the long tiring journey the sides would have to make to play the Boxing Day fixture at Old Trafford. The reserves did play against Bury on Christmas Day, winning 2-0 with goals from Dawson and Doherty.

Supporters were not impressed with the travelling difficulties and the icy, foggy weather, meaning a low crowd of 28,607 for Cardiff's visit on Boxing Day. United were back to a full strength side and, for the fourth consecutive match, were involved in a 3-1 score line as they beat Cardiff thanks to goals from the inside forward trio, Whelan, Taylor and Viollet. All three had also scored heavily in the first half of the season, Whelan leading the way with fourteen goals, although Viollet due to injury curtailing his games was scoring virtually every time he appeared. Tommy Taylor had a great record of scoring against Cardiff, who along with Preston had regularly looked at him when in 1953 he was a Barnsley player. They hesitated; Matt Busby stepped in with a great signing for Manchester United.

Ending the year of 1956, a year which had seen the League title return to Old Trafford, Manchester United travelled to the South coast to play Portsmouth who were in one of the relegation positions. Duncan Edwards showed his complete versatility by taking over the centre forward position from the injured Tommy Taylor and promptly scored one of United's three goals. Pegg and Viollet contributed the other two as, incredibly, United were involved in a fifth 3-1 score line, enabling them to move into 1957 as league leaders. Over at Old Trafford, the reserves also moved confidently into a New Year as they beat West Bromwich 4-1 to move closer to the top of their league with a couple of games in hand.

January 1957
New Years Day 1957 brought a visit from Chelsea with 42,116 watching a comfortable victory 3-0. Tommy Taylor with two and another goal from Dennis Viollet set the tone for a real challenge for the three trophies on offer. One of those trophies, the FA Cup, pitted United with a visit to the North East to play Third Division North Hartlepool United. The previous season had seen a shocking display and defeat at Second Division side Bristol Rovers so everybody was wary of a repeat following. A full house of 17,264 saw United ease into a 3-0 lead and seemingly in the next round. But what a fright and

what a fight Hartlepool put up. They scored just before the half time whistle and had equalised by the 67th minute. The match was already being played on a very heavy pitch and with rain falling for most of the match, the gulf in class was not apparent with twenty minutes to go. It took a late second goal of the game from Billy Whelan to clinch victory. The fans who did not travel to Hartlepool and came to get the score line via the reserves match at Old Trafford saw a fine 4-0 victory over Burnley with Charlton and Dawson amongst the goals again.

Another North East side, this time Newcastle came to Old Trafford and went away totally hammered 6-1 with Whelan, Taylor and Pegg all scoring two each. This was a real fillip for the trip to Spain the following week for the first leg of the quarter final European Cup tie with Bilbao. The reserves travelled to Newcastle and won their eighth game from the last nine by 3-0 to continue their climb up the league table.

Bilbao. Situated in Northern Spain, its people are intensely proud of their Basque heritage which was passionately shown in the Spanish Civil War of 1936-1939. The local football club, Atletico Bilbao, is founded on its policy of playing local Basque people which gives it such a strong feeling of togetherness. Their stadium, the San Mames is named after a Christian thrown to the lions by the Romans who refused to eat him. He was, therefore, made a saint with the ground nicknamed 'The Football Cathedral 'It was into this intense atmosphere, with 45,000 Basques baying for blood, that Matt Busby's 'Babes' entered the fray in January 1957 to play their quarter final 1st leg of the European Cup. Both Bilbao and Manchester United had won their national championships of 1956 although Spain had two sides in these quarter finals as Real Madrid as winners of the first competition were also entered.

Wearing the Blue shirt the club wore to win the 1948 FA Cup Final against Blackpool as Bilbao wore their traditional Red and White stripes, Manchester United took the field in atrocious conditions.

Sunny Spain?
Well, the San Mames stadium was nearly un playable as the two sides entered the field of play. The premise that the further you go in anything the harder it gets was firmly shown to Busby's young side in this match. Bilbao were in front inside the second minute with a goal from inside forward Uribe and when he had added a second and Bilbao a third by half time, Manchester United's excursions in Europe looked like they would be coming to an end. Despite having chances in the first half, United had managed to miss them all and it was with real relief when Tommy Taylor put them on the scoreboard early in the second half. When Viollet scored to make it 3-2, United's hopes were back on track, until this fine Bilbao side moved up a couple of gears and scored twice more to leave the match at 5-2 nearing its end. Then the greatest goal of the match gave hope to Manchester United. Picture the scene, the Spanish senors coasting on the pitch, their fanatical fans making mayhem off it, only ten minutes left, when suddenly Billy Whelan, Manchester United's slim, tall inside right picked up the ball just inside his own half ,

forcing his slight frame through the mud. He beat one man, and then another, where he was getting the strength from nobody knew. Finally, keeping his composure he put the ball past Carmelo in the Bilbao goal to give Manchester United real hope of a comeback in the second leg. For the younger fans, picture Ryan Giggs goal in the semi final against Arsenal at Villa Park. Of all the many goals Billy Whelan was to score for Manchester United none could be as valuable as this, 5-3 made the second leg a realistic chance to overcome the two goal deficit.

The day after this epic match, Manchester United's players had to spend four hours using brushes to free the aircraft of snow and ice, with a real doubt that they would be able to take off. This was a real problem for the club as they had to get back to England to fulfil their fixture on the Saturday against Sheffield Wednesday at Hillsborough. Any delay on that fixture would give real power to the Football League who had been so ferocious in their opposition to Manchester United entering the European Cup in the first place. In the event, the club were able to take off from Bilbao late on the Thursday afternoon, with as they stopped in the Channel Isles at Jersey to refuel, the sun blazing through.

Sheffield Wednesday away before a crowd of 51,068 was always going to be tricky for United after their tiring week and so it proved as despite a goal from Taylor they went down 2-1. Matt Busby employed a full strength side at Sheffield. Where did rotation come from? I am sure there is a valid reason why football clubs have such large squads, but in the 1950's the central league was a strong competition and players not featuring in the first team could get serious games, remember there was no substitutes in those days. It is interesting looking back as why managers continued to play the same side week in week out when they had natural replacements standing by. For example, Manchester United settled on a side as follows; WOOD, FOULKES, BYRNE, COLMAN, JONES, EDWARDS, BERRY, WHELAN, TAYLOR, VIOLLET and PEGG. They had in reserve a replacement for every position except perhaps goalkeeper with such as; GREAVES, BENT, GOODWIN, BLANCHFLOWER, McGUINNESS, WEBSTER, DOHERTY, DAWSON, CHARLTON and SCANLON. This strength in depth was reflected on the same day as the first team lost in Sheffield the reserves beat Wednesday 4-0 at Old Trafford, all of them capable of playing first division football in their own right.

The FA Cup re appeared with a visit to another Third Division North side, Wrexham. A record crowd of 34,445 witnessed United, unchanged yet again, turn the style on with a crushing 5-0 victory with Taylor (2) Whelan (2) and Byrne putting the side in the fifth round and a visit from Everton at Old Trafford. Another victory for the reserves, this time 4-1 against Huddersfield Town put them into third place, six points off the top but with a game in hand.

Chapter NINE

Countdown to chasing Titles and Cups

February 1957

Moving into February Manchester United were top of the league, in the 5th round of the FA Cup, and the quarter finals of the European Cup. They also had this fantastic squad of players, all except Wood, Berry, Taylor and Webster home grown. If Matt Busby's side had started as Babes they were now men...

Maine Road was to be the scene of two matches inside a week, the first a league fixture with City followed by the second leg of the European Cup with Bilbao. 63,872 watched the league match with an unchanged United banishing the Maine Road blues of recent years by winning emphatically 4-2. City caused one or two early problems but goals scored by Whelan, Taylor, Viollet and Edwards kept United four points clear at the top of the table. Over the city at Old Trafford, the reserves won 3-2 thanks to two goals from Alex Dawson, his fifteenth from nineteen games, and one from Bobby Charlton his sixteenth from twenty two games. Everything was in place for the visit of Bilbao now.

Before watching how his side would do in that match, Matt Busby paid a visit down the East Lancashire Road to see his youth side play Everton in the FA Youth tie played in the afternoon. This attention to detail, his knowledge of how all his Manchester United players were doing was part of Matt Busby's success. He must have taken note of his fellow Scotsman Dawson who continued his goal scoring crusade with both United's goals in the 2-2 draw which would bring the sides back to Old Trafford.

Call it hysterical, emotional-anything you like. Manchester will never forget the night United beat Bilbao in the European Cup. Not just beat them but overturn a two goal deficit to win 3-0 on the night thanks to goals from Viollet, Taylor and Berry. The Manchester crowd, because it was a Manchester crowd with even City fans entranced by the United players turning on the skills on their Maine Road pitch, exploded with noise throughout the ninety minutes. Patience was required as Bilbao commanded by their centre half Garay, who was involved in a very physical contest with Tommy Taylor, held out until just before half time when Viollet scored from a rebounded shot from Edwards. When Viollet had two goals, rightly, disallowed inside the first five minutes of the second half the fates seemed against United. The Reds kept going however and a cheeky quick free kick by Colman sent the ball through to Taylor who equalised the tie on the night. European football was decided in these days by playing a third match if the scores were level, when with six minutes left and the crowd still roaring, Taylor and Berry swopped positions for the little winger to slot the winner home. The roar from the near 70,000 crowd could be heard all over Manchester. Nearly sixty years on this is still one of Manchester United's greatest victories.

This was now a very busy time for the team. Back at Old Trafford, welcomed by a crowd of 60,384, United totally destroyed a decent Arsenal side 6-2. Berry (2), Whelan (2), Pegg and Edwards scored the goals, with a young David Herd scoring both Arsenal goals. The team was now playing like a well tuned Rolls Royce, class throughout the side as they marched on over three fronts, including leading the First Division by four points. One disappointment was the reserves suffering a 4-1 defeat away at Liverpool, who themselves were near the top of that league.

The glamour of the FA Cup was on show at Old Trafford with 61,803 seeking revenge for the shock 2-5 league defeat as Everton came to town for the fifth round tie. Albert Dunlop again was in brilliant form denying United's many attacks until with time running out, Duncan Edwards moved through the Everton defence to send a thunderbolt into the bottom corner of the scoreboard end net which not even Dunlop could get to. United made their first change in nine matches with the versatile Colin Webster replacing Johnny Berry.

Within forty eight hours United had to travel to London and play the rearranged match with Charlton Athletic at The Valley. They had to make changes as well with Foulkes (missing his first game of the season) Edwards and Viollet all out. Bobby Charlton returned, again against his namesake side, and went one goal better than his debut match at Old Trafford by scoring a hat trick in United's comfortable 5-1 victory. Tommy Taylor supplied the other two goals as in reality United only had to play at half speed.

For the first time really serious talk was being given to Manchester United becoming the first side this century to win the coveted 'double'. They also had the chance of winning the European Cup, which had immediately become the 'best seller' as far as football crowds were concerned all over Europe, catching the imagination of so many people. That imagination was lifted when the semi final European Cup draw pitted United with the winners of the first years competition, Real Madrid. Whether it was all this talk of possible glory or not but Blackpool, themselves a fine side with such as Stanley Matthews, Jackie Mudie and a young Jimmy Armfield playing for them, slipped into Manchester and beat United 2-0. The reserves at least came back from the seaside with a 1-1 draw.

March 1957
Young players for the future were at the fore as United's youth side played Everton in their youth cup replay. A couple of goals from Dawson were amongst the five United scored as they eased through to the quarter finals for the fifth year 5-2. The link play between Dawson and Mark Pearson was excellent, Pearson knowing the way to goal himself besides his creative play from inside left. Whilst these were under 18's of the future, Old Trafford also staged a schoolboy International trial match between England and The Rest with famous names for the future in Bob Wilson, Norbert Stiles and Bobby Tambling in the England side.

A quarter final tie away at Bournemouth made it three away matches at Third Division North and South teams all posting record crowds wanting to see the greatest side in British football, Manchester United. This time 28,799 turned up at Dean Court with Duncan Edwards reverting to centre forward in the absence of Tommy Taylor who had a bad ankle injury, meaning an FA Cup debut for Wilf McGuinness. Bournemouth had already disposed of Wolverhampton Wanderers and Tottenham Hotspur, when they took the lead and also saw Mark Jones go off with a serious leg injury which would have ramifications for him and United for the rest of the season, hopes were high on the South coast of a serious shock result. Captain Roger Byrne really excelled himself with his leadership and with Duncan Edwards settling into the centre half spot to cover for Jones, United composed themselves. Johnny Berry scored two goals, one a penalty, to earn a semi final place for United for the first time since 1949.

The re arranged mid week match away at Everton produced wholesale changes for United. Foulkes, Colman and Edwards were required to play for The Army whilst Jones and Taylor now had long term injuries, with Viollet also missing this game due to a knock. Reliable replacements in Bent, Goodwin, Blanchflower, McGuinness, Webster and Doherty all stepped in showing the magnificent reserves Busby had. So much so that this much changed team were able to win 2-1 at Goodison Park against a side that had beaten a full strength United side 5-2 earlier in the season at Old Trafford. Colin Webster stepped in for his first league game of the season and promptly scored both goals.

Foulkes, Colman and Edwards were able to return for the visit of Aston Villa, Edwards in the centre forward position with Charlton playing instead of Viollet. Aston Villa were possible FA Cup final opponents for United as they would be in the other semi final against West Bromwich, whilst yet another Midlands side, Birmingham City would face United. All the recent changes and positional switch started to have an effect on United and although the 55,484 crowd gave full support all they had to see was a Bobby Charlton goal to earn a 1-1 draw. The reserves were naturally affected by all the changes as well and they did well to come away from Leeds United also with a 1-1 draw.

A difficult visit before a crowd of 53,228 at Wolverhampton Wanderers produced the same score line and scorer as the week before in a match which saw the debut of twenty year old goalkeeper Gordon Clayton. He had a fine match helping United maintain a comfortable lead at the top of the league. His promotion due to Ray Wood's injury meant David Gaskell was given a match for the reserves at Old Trafford against Bolton Wanderers, his clean sheet helping United to a 1-0 victory.

Manchester United's first semi final for eight years arrived on 23rd March 1957 with Birmingham City the opponents at Hillsborough, home of Sheffield Wednesday. A crowd of 65,107 saw United take the field without Tommy Taylor and Mark Jones both injured and Bobby Charlton and Jackie Blanchflower as their replacements. Birmingham had beaten United just before Christmas so this was not a certainty, but a superb volley from Charlton and a mazy run ending with a low shot into the corner of the net from Berry, against the club he had left to join United in 1951, saw Manchester United at Wembley Stadium for the first time since the great 1948 final against Blackpool. Co incidentally the reserves were playing Aston Villa this day and it was Villa who would be the opponents at Wembley for United in early May. Over at Old Trafford another cup tie, this time the FA Youth cup against Blackburn Rovers was taking place. The spectators had one eye on the scoreboard giving information from Sheffield and the other on a superb display by the next generation of Manchester United. A tremendous 6-0 victory put United into yet another youth cup semi final, with Dawson (2), Lawton and Morgans amongst the goals.

Since September work had been going on with the installation of floodlights at Old Trafford. The rearranged fixture with Bolton Wanderers was the match selected for the much awaited switch on, which duly arrived on Monday 25th March 1957 at 7.30pm. United wearing all red, sadly did not light up the occasion before the expectant 60,862 crowd, losing to Bolton Wanderers for the second time this season 2-0, also the second time without scoring, to their local rivals. As a young lad living just over Trafford Bridge, the night sky was a strange sight as the lights overshadowed not just the famous Old Trafford stadium but the Trafford Park complex of factories. Dennis Viollet dropped out with his injury niggle, with Charlton going to inside left and Edwards back to centre forward, which with the Real Madrid ties on the horizon was worrying for Matt Busby as two of his main strikers were injured.

Having gone three league matches without a victory it was with much relief that United won 2-1 away at Leeds at the end of the month. This match pitted the two Charlton brothers, Bobby and Jack against each other again and it was Bobby with a very late winner who was smiling at the end as Manchester won 2-1. A strong reserve side beat Derby County 2-0 at Old Trafford thanks to two goals from young Shay Brennan which kept them in third place but off the pace to retain the title they had won the season before.

April 1957
The reserves played a quick return with Derby from a match postponed in November and really turned the style on at The Baseball ground by winning 5-1, with the younger members of the side missing as they had a first leg semi final of the FA Youth cup away at Southampton. Going there as the unbeaten champions of over four years, the youth side showed all their ability as they won easily 5-2 at The Dell.

Tottenham Hotspur had been early challengers to United for the championship and even though they had fallen away slightly they still posed a threat to United's chances of retaining their title. The England v Scotland International took place on the same day so Byrne and Edwards were at Wembley helping England to a 2-1 victory. I am sure Tommy Taylor would have been with them but for his ankle injury and Matt Busby held him back with the big Real Madrid match coming the following Thursday in Spain. A 60,349 crowd was reasonably content with a point from a 0-0 draw which made United hot favourites clear at the top of the league with only six fixtures left. The reserves suffered a 2-0 defeat at Wolves, staying in fourth place in their league.

A very important week for the club got off to a shock start when the youth side lost their first ever match in the FA Youth cup on Monday 8th April 1957, as Southampton came to Old Trafford and won 3-2. As United had a three goal lead from the first leg it was not too costly but still a shock to lose for the first time in five years and at Old Trafford. A crowd of 17,000 had no inkling of what was in store as Alex Dawson put United one up on the night, 6-2 on aggregate. That crowd was in shock in the second half as Southampton scored three times without reply. It took another goal from Dawson to make it 2-3 on the night but 7-5 in aggregate in United's favour and a final appearance against West Ham United.

The Manchester United first team party flew off to Madrid on the Tuesday in preparation of their tie with European Cup holders Real Madrid. The match was to be played at the magnificent Bernabeu stadium, a mention of which today still makes me tingle at the thought of one of the greatest stadiums in the world. The tie was played on a Thursday afternoon with an estimated crowd of 135,000 watching as United took the field in all red, ready to match the glamour of the all white kitted Madrid stars. Matt Busby had patched everybody up and went with his strongest side, Jackie Blanchflower still in for Mark Jones. Blanchflower though, was himself a magnificent footballer who stood up to the skills of this fantastic Madrid forward line which read as a football who's who; Kopa, Mateos, Di Stefano, Rial and Gento. Di Stefano was regarded as the world's finest player; Kopa was a French International of great skill, Gento a flying machine on the left wing whilst the two inside forwards Mateos and Rial were Spanish and Argentina Internationals respectively. For the first half United stood firm in the face of some surprising physical antics from Madrid. Into the second half with Taylor magnificent and Pegg running the right back Becerril ragged, United were very much in the game. It took two goals from Rial and Di Stefano mid way through the second half to give Madrid an advantage, only for Taylor to score with less than ten minutes to go and really put United in the driving seat. Sadly, a goal in the closing minutes from Mateos gave Madrid a two goal platform for the second leg although after what United had done to the other Spanish side Bilbao, hopes were really high that Manchester United would be returning to the Bernabeu in late May as the stadium had been honoured with staging the final.

United flew back to London on the Friday in readiness for their fixture at Luton Town on the Saturday. Colman, Whelan and Viollet dropped out for this match but Tommy Taylor showed he was now fully fit again as he scored with a smashing shot and a perfectly timed header to give United a 2-0 victory and one hand firmly on the title. At Old Trafford the reserves beat Barnsley 2-0 and followed it up by beating Blackburn Rovers 3-1 in a rearranged match on the Monday evening.

The busy Easter period confirmed Manchester United's second consecutive league title. The returning Billy Whelan did so in style by scoring a hat trick away at an always difficult

Turf Moor as United beat Burnley 3-1 before a crowd of 41,321.This gave him his twenty fourth goal from thirty six games, with Taylor and Viollet both contributing massively and the young Bobby Charlton scoring ten himself.

Easter Saturday saw the champions play before an Old Trafford crowd of 58,125 who roared their approval as they won 4-0 against Sunderland. Whelan scored a further two goals and Taylor and Edwards completed the easy victory. Bobby Charlton again played instead of Viollet, who like Jones, had suffered lots of injuries this season. Inside the 'United Review' there was a real tribute to the Busby Babes who now surely had outlived that tag. The programme published a specially written calypso in tribute to this fantastic side, the first verse being.

"Manchester, Manchester United A bunch of bouncing Busby Babes they deserve to be knighted. If ever they're playing in your town you must get to that football ground, take a lesson come and see, Football taught by Matt Busby and Manchester, Manchester United, a bunch of bouncing Busby Babes they deserve to be knighted".

The reserves picked up two Easter victories by winning at Sheffield United on Easter Saturday 1-0 and then beat Burnley away on Easter Monday 2-1 as the first team were presented with their trophy with still two matches to go as they entertained Burnley. With the league settled and a vital European Cup semi final due on the Thursday, Matt Busby rotated his side that showed how good they were by beating Burnley 2-0. This was the side that played for United that day; WOOD, FOULKES, GREAVES, GOODWIN, COPE, McGUINNESS, WEBSTER, DOHERTY, DAWSON, VIOLLET and SCANLON. Dennis Viollet was given a virtual fitness test on his persistent groin injury to see if he would be able to get through the Madrid tie, whilst young Alex Dawson, the goal scoring hero for the youth team scored on his United debut with Webster getting the other.

The fixture Manchester United v Real Madrid is still, nearly sixty years on, one of the most magical for the clubs followers. My good friend John Ludden wrote a superb book on the 'Tale of Two Cities' about all the fixtures that have taken place since April 1957.The Manchester match was played on a Thursday evening under the new Old Trafford floodlights, glowing in the night sky over the canal and into Trafford Park from where I lived off Ordsall Lane. That was full of green Salford buses having brought the fans, now waiting to take them back to all points of the city. I walked to the corner of Trafford Bridge and bought the 'United Review' costing 4d (2p) and then came back and played the match with my mates in the street using grids as the goalposts. An interesting point in the programme was on its back cover it showed a map of Europe pin pointing all the sides that had taken place in that seasons competition. As a ten year old it brought all the places you had never heard of to life, and they were played out in your mind on the subbuteo pitch! In later years those were the places I wanted to visit. The match was televised live on Granada, an unusual thing in those days. Still black and white of course, but United were in all dark colours (actually all red) whilst Madrid were in there pristine all white as they took the field before a sold out 65,000. Dennis Viollet was considered unfit so Charlton again played inside left for United. Madrid were not going to sit back like Bilbao and defend their lead they came to play and inside half an hour they had virtually put the tie out of United's reach as goals came from Kopa and Rial. This was Manchester United however, and they responded in the second half with goals from Taylor and Charlton to make the match score 2-2 although the aggregate was 3-5 to Real Madrid who went onto to lift the trophy for a second consecutive year. Going to Cardiff City for an unimportant match from Manchester United's point of view, forty eight hours after the euphoria of a European Cup semi final must have been hard to equate for the side. Cardiff, on the other hand, was fighting for their very survival in the First Division. This was the re arranged fixture from Christmas Day with, surprisingly, only 17,708 people turning out to see the reigning champions and to support the local side in their relegation fight. With an FA Cup Final due the following Saturday, Matt Busby rested five of his starting side, with the team having an average age of twenty two, Alex Dawson making only his second appearance and scoring his second senior goal as United held out for a 1-1 draw which was not good enough for Cardiff who were relegated.

Old Trafford brought its curtain down on a memorable Manchester United season on Monday 29th April 1957, five days before the side had the opportunity to achieve a feat not done this century, winning the 'double' of League and FA Cup. The visitors were West Bromwich Albion for a rearranged fixture from the days of petrol rationing and fog just before Christmas. Matt Busby gave Mark Jones a run out after his long absence and also gave Dennis Viollet another opportunity to claim his spot in the FA Cup Final side. In all, seven reserves were selected and they held a fine West Bromwich side, including Don Howe, Bobby Robson, Ronnie Allen, Derek Kevan and a young Maurice Setters, 1-1 with Alex Dawson scoring for the third time on his third appearance. This left Manchester United with a record number of points in a 42 game season, 64.

Whilst the first team had a cup final to play, the reserves finished their campaign in third position. This left the destiny of the FA Youth cup to be sorted, with West Ham United the opponents over two legs, the first at Upton Park. A crowd of 15,000 expected to see the young Hammers turn over the holders but goals from Dawson, Lawton and Hunter gave United a 3-2 advantage for the second leg. The whole centre of attraction now moved across London from the East end to the North and Wembley Stadium for the FA Cup final.

It was appropriate that the last club to achieve the 'double', Aston Villa, should provide the opposition as this young, vibrant, brilliant Manchester United attempted to do the same all those years after. The expectant 100,000 felt they were in the presence of history being made as United, playing in all white with a red trim, stepped out with an experienced Aston Villa side. In reality, a vicious attack on goalkeeper Ray Wood by Villa's outside left Peter McParland determined the match. With the ball firmly in the hands of Wood, McParland raced from the edge of the area and crashed into him badly injuring his jaw. With no substitutes in those days, Wood was taken off, Jackie Blanchflower putting on the green jersey with Edwards going to centre half. The ten men of United held out marvellously, indeed a far from fit Ray Wood even came back as nuisance value on the wing. As the last half hour approached, the man who should have been sent off after six minutes, Peter McParland turned the knife even more into United by scoring two goals. A late consolation from Taylor was not enough to alter the result and it was Aston Villa who went up for the famous trophy. United's side in the final was; WOOD, FOULKES, BYRNE, COLMAN, BLANCHFLOWER, EDWARDS, BERRY, WHELAN, TAYLOR, CHARLTON and PEGG. For Manchester United, they had another Championship, runners up in the FA Cup and semi finalists in the European Cup. This side was now surely about to not only consolidating its title as England's finest, but also become Europe's top side...

Another trophy was to arrive at Old Trafford, the retaining of the FA Youth Cup. West Ham was no match for the United youngsters as they won 5-0 on the night and 8-2 on aggregate. Seventeen year old Alex Dawson confirmed his emergence as the next star off the pipeline by scoring twice, with Mark Pearson getting two and the captain, outside right Ken Morgans also scoring. All three of these players had real chances of becoming first team players of Manchester United's future. As the season ended, the youths went to Switzerland and won the prestigious Blue Star trophy, whilst the first team, less Byrne and Edwards on International duty and Wood due to his severe injury, went back to Scandinavia and won two friendly matches 3-2 and 4-3.

What would 1957/58 bring to the club?

Chapter TEN
On the Brink of Immortality

Having sewn up two consecutive titles, had a real crack at both the FA and European Cups, surely this was to be the season when at least a double would be achieved, and with the squad they had, a possible treble.

Manchester in 1957, twelve years on from the end of the war, was starting to come to life entertainment wise. The main cinemas, one of the biggest entertainment outlets, were the Gaumont, the Odeon and the Theatre Royal. Younger people now were suddenly being called teenagers and they had music and dancing outlets such as The Ritz and The Plaza, whilst the older crowd has such as the Bodega and night clubs such as the Sportsman and the Cromford Club. Not that the wages Manchester United players got meant they were rolling in money, in 1957 the maximum wage was £15 per week plus £2 appearance money and a £3 win bonus. The Busby Babes were now getting recognised constantly in Manchester, whilst they were filling grounds regularly when they were the visitors.

August 1957

Normally the pre season match Manchester United was involved with was the public practice game between The Reds and The Blues. With Europe now on the agenda, it was decided to take in a couple of pre season fixtures in Germany in Berlin and Hannover. A 3-0 victory in Berlin and 4-2 in Hannover both games giving the British troops much to cheer. Dennis Viollet was, hopefully, back to full fitness as he showed a fine goal scoring touch with four of the goals, Tommy Taylor scoring the other three in these matches.

It was their inside forward partner though, Billy Whelan, who stole all the headlines on the opening days fixture at newly promoted Leicester City, before a full house of 40,214 many United fans amongst them. Billy scored an hat trick as United started the season in style with a 3-0 away victory. He became only the second Manchester United player to score an hat trick on the first day of the season, Jack Rowley being the other, although Bobby Charlton and Lou Macari equalled this feat since. A former Manchester United star inside right was playing for Leicester in this match, Johnny Morris and he marvelled at how well United played as they looked to equal the feat of Huddersfield Town and Arsenal in winning three titles on the trot. Manchester United started the season with the following side; WOOD, FOULKES, BYRNE, COLMAN, BLANCHFLOWER, EDWARDS, BERRY, WHELAN, TAYLOR, VIOLLET and PEGG. Only two of those players would play in the last match of the season...

The reserves also started their season in real style as they beat Blackburn Rovers 5-1 at Old Trafford. Included in the side were Mark Jones, Bobby Charlton, Albert Scanlon, and young goal scoring sensation Alex Dawson who scored two of the goals. Monday brought a very surprising defeat for the reserves in their away fixture at Everton, losing 3-1, as the two senior sides prepared to meet at Old Trafford on the Wednesday , 59,103 turned out to welcome the consecutive season champions and were well rewarded as United turned on the style and won comfortably 3-0. An Everton own goal started the scoring with Taylor and Viollet then getting in on the act.

An even bigger attendance turned up on the last day of August to witness the Manchester Derby with City. 63,347 packed out Old Trafford to see a convincing display from United as they won 4-1 thanks to goals from Berry, Edwards, Taylor and Viollet. It was particularly good to see how well Dennis Viollet had returned from his persistent groin injury at the end of the previous season which cost him his Cup Final place. The man who replaced him in that final, Bobby Charlton, was on the score sheet for the reserves over at Maine Road as they got back on track after their mid week defeat with a 4-3 victory. Albert Scanlon scoring the winner in the last minute before a crowd of over 12,000.

September 1957
The topsy turvy display of the reserves was highlighted on the Monday when Everton came to Old Trafford and completed a quick league double by winning 4-2. Indeed, Everton were 4-1 up at half time which did not impress the almost 13,000 crowd. This was a couple of surprising results because United had a very strong side out in both games. Certainly the football public was responding to the style of football Manchester United were playing as was shown by the enormous crowd at Goodison Park for the Everton return fixture, 72,077 packing out the ground. They were well rewarded with a fantastic match which saw a 3-3 draw, United's first dropped point of the season as Berry, Whelan and Viollet scored the goals.

My late father Albert had a bad time in the Second World War at the hands of the Japanese being a prisoner of war since his capture in Singapore. His time on the Burma railways was not one to be repeated and for many years after that war he suffered many ills. It was, therefore, my mother Hilda who joined me for the Leeds United match in early September 1957. It was not without incident, as we crossed the Trafford Road swing bridge with many others, as cars were not that prominent in those days, when with a boat approaching, the bridge was closed all passengers still on it, as it turned to allow the boat to pass. On we went, gaining admission high up in the paddock alongside the main stand at the scoreboard end of the ground with 50,842 other supporters. Leeds had lost the services of their magnificent player John Charles, who had joined Juventus for £65,000, and this Manchester United side was in no mood for leniency as they swept the Yorkshire side aside 5-0. Berry (2), Taylor (2) and Viollet being the scorers. Over in Yorkshire, the reserves managed their third victory to go with their two defeats as they beat Leeds 3-1, Alex Dawson with two of them.

The reserves had their first draw when Blackpool held them 2-2 at Old Trafford, but on the same night in the seaside resort with the illuminations in full flow, United's first team scored a tremendous 4-1 victory in front of a full house 34,181. Still unbeaten, still unchanged, five wins and one draw kept United clear at the top of the table thanks to goals from Whelan(2) and Viollet(2). If anybody was going to stop this United side it would be Bolton Wanderers, and so it was when the sides met at Burnden Park on Saturday 14th September. Just as the praise had been flowing in the press after the marvellous victory at Blackpool, they were all of the opinion that United were not the same side of the previous two seasons as they lost heavily 4-0.It still left United at the top of the table however so some of the comments were premature, as perhaps they are today when Manchester United lose a match. For the second consecutive match the reserves drew 2-2, this time at Old Trafford against Bolton with John Doherty getting both the goals.

There was a lot of interesting comments in the 'United Review' for the visit of Blackpool with information given that 172,000 had watched the three home matches so far, and that all the away games had been sells outs reflecting the lure of this fantastic side. The programme also noted that a England and Manchester schoolboy International had joined the playing staff by the name of Norbert Stiles, soon to be shortened to Nobby, and that besides playing in the junior sides he was helping out in the club offices. In later years as I had the pleasure of meeting Nobby at various events he recalled the time he went to Old Trafford to sign for the club. His father was an undertaker and Nobby remembered being driven to meet Jimmy Murphy in a hearse! According to the programme you also had the chance to meet Matt Busby the following Saturday at the main book shop in Manchester, Sherratt & Hughes to buy his new book 'My Story'. All these good stories was not reflected on the pitch as Blackpool came to town and inflicted a surprise defeat on United,2-1, only a week after being hammered at home. The reserves went goal mad at the seaside winning 8-1 as they finally reflected their ability in results. They would now be the team to beat in their league.

Having signed his books in Manchester in the morning, Matt Busby showed his usual calm manner in not reacting wildly to the two successive defeats for his championship side and kept faith with them as Arsenal arrived at Old Trafford. Arsenal were still one of the glamour names of English football and United, of course, was trying to emulate their achievement of, along with Huddersfield Town, of winning three consecutive league titles. The United team responded with a 4-2 victory turning in one of their finest displays of the season. Whelan (2), Taylor and Pegg all amongst the goals, with young David Herd again scoring against United for Arsenal.

This was a perfect platform for United as the European Cup appeared on the agenda the following Wednesday with a very short trip across the Irish Sea to play Shamrock Rovers in Dublin. In 1957 there was not the same sort of information about players, if you had heard of them with so little television in the Emerald Isle; people had not actually seen these figures. They knew all about one Manchester United player though, Liam Whelan giving him his Irish name. Known as Billy, to all Mancunians, he had told his team mates how good this Shamrock Rovers side was so you can imagine the astonishment as Manchester United promptly won 6-0 before a full house of 45,000. It was a wild Dublin night with a roaring gale seeing United 1-0 up at half time, and with the wind behind them! Because of the terrible conditions there was only a two minute half time change around and it was Billy who found his goal scoring feet with goals in the 51st and 56th minute which settled the tie. Three late goals made the 0-6 score line a bit harsh on Shamrock Rovers but at least the Dubliners went home happy that their local lad had proved his worth in this magnificent Manchester United side.

Once back in Manchester, Matt Busby was left with a severe illness outbreak amongst his players. Eddie Colman had dropped out against Shamrock, the first change in the tenth fixture, with Freddie Goodwin stepping in. Faced with a top of the table match against Wolverhampton Wanderers there was seven fitness doubts as the team bus left for the Midlands. Eventually, besides Colman, Byrne, Whelan and Viollet all missed out whilst Wood, Blanchflower, Berry and Taylor only just passed fitness tests. With injuries and illness also to Greaves and Bent it was Wilf McGuinness who was pressed into the left back position. It was no surprise, therefore as Wolves were too strong on the day for United winning 3-1 with John Doherty getting United's consolation goal. This defeat took United off the top of the table for the first time in a very long while. I have an interesting single sheet programme from the reserves fixture that day at Old Trafford. With all the illness about, the United side shows six changes whilst the Villa team had ten changes! United made it an even worse day for Villa as they won 6-1 to go top of the table.

October 1957

It was the return of European football to Old Trafford first week in October 1957, although the visitors were from only across the Irish Sea, Shamrock Rovers. Trailing 0-6 it was always going to be a difficult night for them, although United were missing Edwards, Blanchflower and the hero of the first tie, Ireland's new star Billy Whelan. The crowd was the smallest that had attended a European home match 33,754 and they saw a much closer game with United winning 3-2 and 9-2 on aggregate, Viollet(2) and Pegg getting the United goals.

FA Cup Final opponents from the previous season, Aston Villa, arrived at Old Trafford for the first of two visits inside a fortnight. The first was a league fixture the second would be the Charity Shield. United put out a similar side as in that final, although Mark Jones came back at centre half as Jackie Blanchflower was playing for Northern Ireland against Scotland and with Edwards still unfit, Wilf McGuinness was at left half. Revenge was not really a word Matt Busby would want to use but he must have wanted his side to win this match more than most. They did not disappoint, and helped by an own goal, one from Pegg and two from Tommy Taylor United won 4-1 and kept them close to the top of the table. The reserves were already at that position in their league, even a surprise 4-2 defeat at Derby County not affecting that spot.

Nottingham Forest had been promoted this season, and for United's second visit to the East Midlands, they again provided a full house, this time a record with 47,654 inside the City Ground with many alongside the actual pitch as the police looked to keep control. Forest had made a great start to the season and was actually up with United just behind the two West Midland clubs, Wolves and West Bromwich Albion. United wearing their cup final all white strip of the previous season turned on a great display helped by the return of Edwards and Blanchflower. Goals from Whelan and Viollet secured a 2-1 victory. Back at Old Trafford United reserves beat their nearest challenger, Sheffield Wednesday 3-0 to stay clear at the top.

The clash with the Wales v England International match at Cardiff decimated the Manchester United side for the visit of Portsmouth in mid October 1957. Byrne, Edwards and Taylor had all been selected, with Dawson, McGuinness and a debut for Peter Jones at left back as their replacements. This was a match, however, against a poor Portsmouth side who had not won for eight matches, so you can imagine the real shock for the 38,253 crowd, myself amongst them, as Portsmouth won 3-0 with a young Derek Dougan having an outstanding match for them at centre forward. In the 'United Review' for this match was a sign of how difficult it was to arrange European fixtures in those days, as Manchester United would be travelling behind the Iron Curtain for the first time with a visit to Prague to play Dukla. They had not appeared at the draw and so to communicate the dates for the two legged tie, Manchester United had to send letters to Prague to try and fix dates! At least the reserves were on the right side of a 3-0 score line, winning away at Burnley.

Aston Villa returned to Old Trafford for the second time in seventeen days, this time for the Charity Shield. A surprisingly low crowd of 27,293 saw confirmation of United's superiority over Villa as they won 4-0, such a pity that this could not have been Wembley five months earlier. Freddie Goodwin replaced Colman in an otherwise full United side who therefore retained the Charity Shield. The FA Youth cup started again with United off to Burnley as they sought to win the competition for the sixth successive season. A much changed side from the previous season still included Dave Gaskell in goal who had played in the first team, Mark Pearson who had forged a brilliant link with Alex Dawson the last season, Nobby Lawton and John Giles, making his FA Youth cup debut. Lawton scored one of United's two goals which won the tie 2-0.

When Manchester United loses a match it seems the whole world wants an answer. When they lost for the fifth time this season, and the second in a row, at West Bromwich Albion it was however, in a seven goal thriller which is still talked about in the West Midlands. In 1988 (reprinted in 1999) Iain McCartney and I wrote the biography of Duncan Edwards and we were honoured to have Bobby (later Sir) Robson write the foreword. Bobby played in that match for West Brom who won 4-3, Johnny Berry missing a penalty at 3-2, with Taylor (2) and Whelan getting the goals. Bobby felt that it was the best match he had ever played in but from Manchester United's point of view their form was not as fluent as it had been in the first matches of the season. Back at Old Trafford the reserves stayed clear at the top of the table as they hammered Preston North End 6-1 including a surprising scorer in Bobby Harrop. He had been a regular at centre and left half but had to be played at inside forward due to the recent illness and injury situation. He responded brilliantly by scoring a hat trick in this Preston match, his seventh goal in five reserve appearances!

Chapter ELEVEN

Times they are a Changing

As we move into the month of November, nobody realised we were moving into a three month spell which would signal not only an end of one of the greatest sides the world has seen, but a defining time for Manchester United for the rest of their existence...

November 1957

A near 50.000 crowd welcomed Burnley to Old Trafford hoping to see Manchester United get back to winning ways in the league. Goodwin was still at number four for Eddie Colman with Colin Webster coming in at number ten as Viollet missed out again with the ankle injury he sustained against Villa in the Charity Shield. The crowd went home quite relieved as at least United managed a 1-0 victory thanks to a Tommy Taylor goal to stop the mini losing league run. Interestingly, the 'United Review' discussed the arrangements for the forthcoming European Cup tie against Dukla Prague. In those early days of the competition there was no set date and clubs had to arrange the matches themselves. Whilst Dukla were quite happy to come to Old Trafford on 20th November they wanted the second leg to be played on a Saturday or a Sunday in Prague as they had poor floodlights and they did not think their fans would be able to get to an afternoon mid week fixture. Obviously, United had to play league fixtures on the days Dukla proposed so they went to work to improve their lighting system. Bobby Harrop continued his goal scoring form for the reserves by scoring two in a 5-0 victory at Newcastle, Charlton(2) and Scanlon with the other goals.

Those last two named, Charlton and Scanlon got the goals at Old Trafford when Liverpool arrived for the Central League fixture. The 2-1 victory also saw the return from injury of Eddie Colman at right half. Alex Dawson missed the reserve match as he was called into the FA Youth cup side as they travelled to Blackpool, making a fine impression by scoring five goals as United won 7-0. Freddie Goodwin continued to deputise for Eddie as the first team travelled to Preston North End where a full house of 39,063 saw the sides play out a 1-1 draw with Billy Whelan getting the United goal.

Wednesday 13th November should have seen the first leg of the European Cup tie at Old Trafford against Dukla Prague but the sudden death of the Czechoslovakian President meant the Czech side had to return home at short notice and the match was put back a week. Sheffield Wednesday visited Old Trafford on Saturday 16th November with the 'United Review' showing action on the cover of the previous weeks match at Preston. What was interesting for future years was the involvement of Preston wing half Frank O'Farrell as he got caught between his own goalkeeper and Tommy Taylor. Eddie Colman made his welcome return to the side, two years after his debut, this was his ninety first appearance to show how far he had come, along with two league championship medals, and he was able to celebrate another victory as two Colin

Webster goals won the match 2-1 for the defending champions. A 3-0 victory for the reserves at Stoke maintained their fine form.

A full house at Old Trafford under the floodlights brings a special atmosphere and that was the case as Dukla Prague arrived a week after the original date. They were effectively the Czech army side but they were no mugs and in Josef Masopust at left half they had a world class performer. The first half was scoreless and it took another goal from Colin Webster after sixty three minutes to open the tie up. Taylor quickly made it two nil and David Pegg finished it off with a great shot for United to take a 3-0 score line on their long trip to Prague in a couple of week's time.

Johnny Berry picked up a knock in the European match so Albert Scanlon came in at outside right for the visit to Newcastle. Albert was a natural left winger but he had been excellent for the reserves all season and fully deserved his chance. United had a full house of 54,000 Geordies to contend with along with a fired up Newcastle side but they continued their improved form with a fine 2-1 victory, Duncan Edwards and Tommy Taylor scoring the goals. Back at Old Trafford it was goals that were making the news there with the reserves scoring another five to take their total to sixty six from eighteen games as they beat West Bromwich Albion 5-1 to go five points clear at the top of the league.

I was at Old Trafford the following Saturday to see Tottenham Hotspur. They were struggling in mid table, and with United only five points off the top and a game in hand, this was a great opportunity to consolidate their position. At half time it was 1-4 to Tottenham! United suffered illness and injury problems on the day of the game with Ray Wood dropping out to give sixteen year old David Gaskell his full debut, although he had, of course, come on as a substitute in the previous season Charity Shield. Tommy Taylor also missed out along with Berry and Viollet's continued absence, and Bobby Smith the Tottenham centre forward took full advantage with a first half hat trick. Two goals from Pegg and one from Whelan did make the final score a respectable 3-4 but this was a worrying defeat for Matt Busby for he hoped to win a third consecutive championship.

December 1957
A trip behind the Iron Curtain to play the second leg against Dukla in Prague was cushioned by a three goal advantage and also the return of Ray Wood and Mark Jones who replaced Jackie Blanchflower after his mauling by Bobby Smith the previous Saturday. Despite going behind after seventeen minutes and having what seemed a decent equaliser from Taylor ruled out, United now were aware of the European experience and held onto a 3-1 aggregate victory to move into the quarter finals. The return air trip to Manchester caused one or two problems however, when it was learned that both Manchester and London airports were fog bound so the team re routed to Amsterdam. En route to Manchester from there they learned they would have to be directed to Liverpool airport getting back in Manchester at around 11pm on the Friday

night. It was then off to Birmingham the following morning to play at St Andrews against the local City side.

Dennis Viollet had been injured for a few matches, so it was very welcoming to see his return at Birmingham and he was immediately back in the goals with two of United's three, Taylor getting the other goal. Problem was that Birmingham City also scored three in a high scoring draw. Viollet's return allowed Matt Busby to play what was the accepted Manchester United team; WOOD, FOULKES, BYRNE, COLMAN, JONES, EDWARDS, BERRY, WHELAN, TAYLOR, VIOLLET and PEGG. The free scoring reserve side achieved a comfortable 4-0 victory over Bury at Old Trafford with Albert Scanlon continuing his fine form with two goals.

That line up noted above as the accepted Busby Babes team were to play together for the last time against Chelsea at Old Trafford. A crowd of just fewer than 37,000 witnessed another home defeat to a London side, this time 1-0. Chelsea, like Tottenham the previous home match were floating around in mid table and although they were regularly under pressure only to break away and score a goal with five minutes to go. This, no doubt, was now a problem for Matt Busby who saw his champions in third place, ten points behind Wolves although with a game in hand. It was not a great day all round for the club as the reserves suffered their first defeat in ten matches having won all nine of the previous matches at Huddersfield. There was mitigating circumstances however, as both Ian Greaves and Jackie Blanchflower both suffered injuries with United two goals up. Huddersfield sensed their opportunity and scored four times without further reply. This defeat cut the reserves lead to three points.

Alex Dawson missed the reserve match at Huddersfield due to an injury but was fit for the mid week FA Youth Cup tie at Leeds United. He came back with a bang, scoring a hat trick as United cruised through 4-1.

Matt Busby had decisions to make and true to the man, he made them bringing goalkeeper Harry Gregg from Doncaster Rovers for a world record fee for a goalkeeper, and also decided to shake up his forward line by dropping Johnny Berry, Billy Whelan and David Pegg in favour of Kenny Morgans, Bobby Charlton and Albert Scanlon for the visit of Leicester City. Morgans and Charlton was a real testimony to the continued youth policy of Matt Busby. These changes were unusual for United as Matt Busby kept a tight ship and unless International calls or injury intervened he picked his best side. Simple! He was rewarded immediately with a crushing 4-0 victory thanks to two goals from Viollet and one each from Charlton and Scanlon. A new look Manchester United was ready to do battle on all three fronts again. The reserves quickly got back to winning ways with a 4-1 victory at Blackburn Rovers.

Question. Would you go to a football match on Christmas Day?
Until December 25th 1957 that was an accepted part of the way of life. It was also the last time that it has happened though for Manchester United, and I was fortunate enough to have been there, and still remember most of it!

Luton Town was the opposition that day with a Manchester United side carrying an average age of 23.Two of the side was actually only making their second appearance for the club, Harry Gregg the charismatic goalkeeper just signed from second division Doncaster Rovers for that record fee after his sensational display the month before for his native Northern Ireland against England at Wembley, when the Irish had won a famous victory 3-2. The other player making only his second appearance was young Welshman Kenny Morgans continuing his place on the right wing in favour of Johnny Berry. Christmas Day 1957 I was ten. My late father Albert went with me to the match and it was always great to be with him. My upbringing was great because you knew nothing different. The old Docks, now Media City, the BBC, and futuristic Quays, dominated Trafford Road where we walked to Old Trafford. I vividly remember men standing outside the Dock gates every day, waiting for a possible day's work, hoping a foreman would offer it to them. They sold the programme, the 'United Review' on Trafford Bridge, the Luton issue costing the normal 4d (2p). I collected programmes most of my life, having all but four of United's homes at one stage. Imagine in later years having the real honour of writing in that programme in the late 1970's early 80's including the famous Barcelona 3-0 match. Happy Days!

The kick off this last Christmas Day fixture was 2.45pm, even though floodlights had now arrived at Old Trafford nine months earlier. We stood in the old paddock running from the players tunnel centre line towards the Stretford End. As you looked around the stadium, both ends were uncovered, the Stretford End stretching right back whilst the other end only had the old scoreboard at its back. Joining the two ends was a massive standing area with only a roof going from penalty area to penalty area, and then you came to where I was in front of the main stand which was covered. Football crowds varied massively in this time, 25,000 or 60,000, this match there was 39,444 including me and my dad. Jack Crompton was the Luton trainer this day, not long since having been the Manchester United goalkeeper. Within two months he would be back at Old Trafford due to an unimaginable disaster. Manchester United had got the confidence back the previous match and comfortably beat Luton 3-0 thanks to a goal each from Edwards, Taylor and Charlton. The last Manchester United line up for a Christmas Day fixture was; GREGG, FOULKES, BYRNE, COLMAN, JONES, EDWARDS, MORGANS, CHARLTON, TAYLOR, VIOLLET and SCANLON.

A very experienced reserve side including Wood, Blanchflower, Berry, Whelan and Pegg was held at Old Trafford on Boxing Day by Barnsley 3-3 but still lead their table. The same day the first team had travelled south to play the return fixture with Luton in front of a full house of 26,438 who witnessed a much closer match than I had the day before as the sides played out a 2-2 draw, Scanlon and Taylor getting the United goals.

Having played on Wednesday and Thursday, United played their third match in four days when they crossed Manchester to play local rivals City before a massive 70,483 crowd. They suffered a blow before kick off with Tommy Taylor dropping out to be replaced by the very useful Colin Webster.This turned out to be one of the great 'derby's' as City went hammer and tong with their successful neighbour. Dennis Viollet, a Manchester lad, scored in his sixth successive match against City, with young Bobby Charlton scoring in his first match against them. City scored two themselves and honours ended even, with new goalkeeper Harry Gregg showing a different side to Ray Wood by coming for every cross, Ray used to be more of a line goalkeeper. A couple of times Harry clattered his own defenders who shook their heads and just said,'keep coming big man!' Over the city in the reserve match, United won easily 4-0 with yet another hat trick from Alex Dawson who was shurely going to be a big star of the future.

January 1958

As Manchester United moved into 1958 they were slightly off the pace for a third successive Championship, about to start their FA Cup challenge and looking forward to a quarter final European Cup tie with Red Star Belgrade. Matt Busby's signing of goalkeeper Harry Gregg was his first signing since Tommy Taylor in 1953 and he was in a very good mood talking about the future. "In all modesty my summing up of 1955/56 and 1966/57 must be that no club in the country could live with Manchester United"

The whole club could not be in a much better shape really, the reserves were clear at the top of their league whilst the youth team continued to be the team to beat in their competition, defending the trophy they had won in its first five seasons of existence. Indeed, the first match of 1958 at Old Trafford was the FA Youth Cup tie with Newcastle United on Saturday 4th January. This was also the start of the FA Cup and the first team were up at Borough Park in Workington, playing a Third Division side at this stage for the second successive season.

The youth side gave a great display in front of over 19,000, with Nobby Stiles and John Giles having excellent matches, although it was the deadly partnership of Alex Dawson and Mark Pearson who scored the majority of the goals in an emphatic 8-0 victory, Dawson with four and Pearson with three. Up at Workington, following the disastrous defeat at Bristol Rovers two years before and the close call at Hartlepool last season, it was a wary Manchester United who travelled north. They had cause to be wary as Workington in front of a full house 21,000 went 1-0 up at half time. This news relayed back to the Old Trafford crowd watching the youth side did get better though in the second half as Dennis Viollet turned in a brilliant performance to score a hat trick and put the side into the 4th round as they aimed to get back to Wembley after last season's disappointment. Incidentally, on a busy day for the club, the reserves with a strong side out despite the youth match, incredibly lost 6-5 at Barnsley but still topped the table.

Dennis Viollet was on the goal sheet the week after as United played their fourth successive away fixture, this time at Leeds United. The match finished at 1-1, the third consecutive draw for the team in the First Division. United played really well in the first half but were pushed all the way in the second, hanging on for the draw at the end. Over at Old Trafford, the reserves brushed off their poor showing at Barnsley by scoring five for the second successive match, this time restricting their opponents, Leeds, to three. Following Matt Busby's shake up just before Christmas this was a very strong side with David Pegg scoring a first half hat trick. Johnny Berry and Alex Dawson scored the other two which put United four points clear of Wolves.

The return of European football came to Old Trafford on the unusual night of Tuesday the 14th January as Red Star Belgrade came into town. There was a real doubt about the match going ahead as the pitch was rock hard and the Manchester fog enveloped the stadium. I remember the match being televised live and it being very difficult on the black and white telly to make out what was going on. Red Star had a very good side with a tremendous goalkeeper in Vladimir Beara playing in an all black kit,and a superb inside forward called Dragoslav Sekularac. It was his brilliant prompting which enabled Red Star to take the lead. I mentioned earlier that Harry Gregg liked to dominate his area and he claimed later that with the fog swirling around he did not see Tasic's lob from about thirty yards as it sailed over his head. This young Manchester United side, average age 23, fought back brilliantly in the second half with goals from Bobby Charlton and a late winner from Eddie Colman, only his second ever goal for the team. It was still a close call however and the 60,000 crowd knew their side would be up against it in Belgrade for the second leg in three weeks time.

United v. Red Star—14th January, 1958   Photo by courtesy of the Daily Mail
Red Star's goalkeeper Beara makes a leaping silhouette against the floodlights as he is beaten by a fast, low shot from Charlton (extreme left) who had taken a pass from Taylor. On a hard but slippery pitch United hit two goals against a single from Red Star in the fog-bound but thrilling second round European Cup Match.

It was time now for the team to turn those draws into victories and get closer to Wolverhampton Wanderers at the top of the tale, particularly with a meeting between the two due in early February at Old Trafford. The visit of Bolton Wanderers however was not going to make that an easy option as they were a distinctly difficult side for United to beat in recent years. United though were in very good form with their newly formed attack now gaining more confidence. This was fully proved on the day when they turned in an exceptional display to beat a very good Bolton side 7-2 with Bobby Charlton scoring a hat trick, Dennis Viollet two, one from Scanlon and a net busting penalty from Duncan Edwards. Penalty takers have their own ideas on the perfect penalty, in Edwards's case he always went for the same option, run in hard and belt the thing straight down the middle. Indeed, the opposing goalkeeper needed to dive to get out of the way! With Wolves losing at Blackpool, United now had them firmly in their sights. Billy Whelan had lost his place to Bobby Charlton and showed his determination of getting back into the side by scoring both the reserves goals at Bolton, although the match ended 2-2.

I went to my first ever FA Cup tie on 25th January as second division Ipswich Town, managed by Alf Ramsey came to Old Trafford. My dad took me in the paddock alongside the main stand side, I can still remember seeing the snow piled up against the wooden pickets which ran around the ground. Ipswich had Roy Bailey in their goal, his son Gary later to be a top player in the same position for Manchester United. United were in top form right now, unbeaten in eight, soon to be nine as Bobby Charlton scored both goals in a 2-0 victory. It was also announced that Matt Busby would be Scotland's manager for the forthcoming summer World Cup finals in Sweden, joining his magnificent assistant Jimmy Murphy who would be leading Wales. Everything looked rosy for the club as we moved into February 1958.

How soon can hopes disappear?

Chapter TWELVE
February 1958

Saturday 1st February 1958

A visit to London to play mid table Arsenal gave Manchester United a real chance to get closer to Wolverhampton Wanderers, especially with the sides having to meet at Old Trafford the following Saturday. Bearing in mind that on the Wednesday in between United had to play Red Star in Belgrade, it is interesting that in those days there was never a thought to give players a rest or use rotation of what was after all a very large experienced pool of players.

The trip got off to a very sombre start with the death of one of the clubs three directors who operated under the chairmanship of Harold Hardman. George Whittaker, at 82 the oldest of those three directors, died suddenly in the team's hotel in central London on the morning of the match. Both the sides wore black arm bands as a sign of respect, with a couple of pictures from the start of the match used regularly over the years. One shows Captain Roger Byrne sweeping out of the Highbury tunnel, ball in both hands as he led his team out. The other picture is also poignant in that it shows Duncan Edwards signing an autograph on the Highbury pitch with the famous Highbury clock showing just a couple of minutes to kick off. The happenings the following week make these pictures dramatic, sad but also a vivid reminder of how special these players and team were...

Wearing all white, United swept forward with a classic display which enthralled the sold out Highbury crowd of 63,578.Kenny Morgans was quickly in the action causing full back Evans early problems. It was from one of Morgans raids after ten minutes that he cut the ball back for Duncan Edwards to run onto from about twenty yards and send a cracking shot into the bottom corner of Arsenal's net. Arsenal settled after this and led by centre forward David Herd they started to cause problems for Harry Gregg in the United goal. Albert Scanlon on the opposite wing to Morgans , turned in one of his best matches for the club and with both wingers starting to push Arsenal back it was no surprise after an half hour when Bobby Charlton moved onto a Scanlon cross and hammered in the second goal.

A disallowed goal from Arsenal for offside, was complimented by a strong appeal for a United penalty before what seemed would be a decisive third goal arrived just as the half time whistle was about to blow. Morgans again was the provider sending over a cross for Tommy Taylor to bundle over the line after a strange barren spell for United's centre forward, this being his first goal for five matches. 0-3 at half time was a comforting score with a busy week forthcoming.

Early in the second half Duncan Edwards showed his muscle as he crashed into Arsenal inside forward Derek Tapscott leaving him in a heap. Denis Evans the Arsenal full back was incensed at what he considered an over the top tackle by Duncan. He thought at the time that he would get his revenge on Duncan if the opportunity arose, and in later life after the happenings of the next week or so, often wished he had. Evans often thought that if he had done Duncan, as he perceived Duncan had done his mate, then he might not have been able to go to Belgrade the following week and the course of the history of one of Manchester United's greatest ever players might have been changed.

As the second half started with Arsenal 0-3 down, few of the packed out crowd could have known that within fifteen minutes the scores would have been level. David Herd got the first and Jimmy Bloomfield helped himself to two as the Highbury crowd went wild. With the floodlights now on the atmosphere inside Highbury was also of an electric nature. Even though Roger Byrne took a knock which seemed to be causing him concerns ,United grew again and both the wingers, Morgans and Scanlon, continued to be causing Arsenal problems. First Scanlon provided the cross for Viollet to put United 4-3 up then Morgans provided the opening for Taylor to get his second, and United's fifth of the afternoon. Arsenal came back themselves with their fourth goal from Tapscott with ten minutes left but United held out for a vital victory which left them in a decent position near the top of the table.

As the sides pulled themselves off the Highbury pitch with the crowd giving tremendous applause to both sides, nobody could realise that this would be the last time five of the Manchester United players would ever be seen again on a British football pitch...

It was a very happy team travelling back to Manchester on the Saturday night with some of the lads intending to have a bit of a party in places such as the Plaza or more sophisticated places like the Cromford Club. Everything in the garden was rosy surely?

On this same Saturday 1st February, I was at Old Trafford with 19,000 other supporters watching a star studded reserves side play a top of the table match with Wolverhampton Wanderers. Ray Wood, Geoff Bent ,Jackie Blanchflower, Johnny Berry, Billy Whelan and David Pegg all were in the United side, with Ron Flowers who was to become an England International playing for Wolves. United took the lead with a goal from Colin Webster after he was set up by Billy Whelan, but Flowers equalised then Wolves went 2-1 up at half time. I remember roaming around the ground as you could in those days, standing in different positions. United came out fighting in the second half and Alex Dawson equalised before David Pegg scored twice, once from the penalty spot. Close to the end Wolves pulled a goal back but United finished up 4-3 winners and a three point lead with a game in hand, at the top of the Central League.

Sunday 2nd February 1958
Ted Dalton the club physiotherapist took centre stage on the Sunday morning as those with knocks and bumps were checked out. Wilf McGuinness was one hoping his recent injury would be signed off to get a last minute call up the next day but he was still not ready for a return. Jimmy Murphy and Matt Busby had last minute discussions on the way they should tackle the threat of Red Star.

Monday 3rd February 1958

There had been one or two alterations to the United travelling party to Belgrade as Colin Webster went down with flu and as Roger Byrne had received a knock at Arsenal, Geoff Bent was included instead of Ronnie Cope who had expected to go. The team met up at Old Trafford and travelled the short distance to Manchester Airport on a cold, damp depressing Monday morning with Jimmy Murphy not with his beloved side as he was off to Israel managing the Wales team as they tried to qualify for the World Cup Finals in Sweden, Bert Whalley taking his place on the flight. Fog was also in the Manchester air this Monday as the team was delayed before its six hour flight, via Munich, to Belgrade. The flight was via a chartered Elizabethan as the club were conscious they could not rely on the scheduled services as they needed to be back in Manchester in good time for their important match with Wolves on the Saturday.

Tuesday 4th February 1958

The Second World War was now thirteen years in the past, although rationing was not that long a thing of the past in Manchester. What the team saw when they arrived in Belgrade, however, genuinely shocked most. All around was armed soldiers wandering the streets, even the floors of the hotel Metropole had their presence on each floor. I remember Dennis Viollet saying in the book Brian Hughes MBE and myself wrote called 'VIOLLET' how shocked the team was. "It had been snowing and the place was very cold, yet people were walking around with no shoes, even those who had something on their feet it was from old tyres as makeshift footwear. There was no queue in the shops as they were virtually empty of stuff. Of course, this was only a couple of years after the uprising in Hungary, and many on this trip thought if this was communism you can keep it".

Wednesday 5th February 1958

The weather was freezing cold and there were doubts about the match actually going ahead, but the morning of the game saw the sun out and the pitch was thawing when the players arrived at the stadium in readiness for the 2.45 kick off. In a replica of the Arsenal match United stormed into action and had blown Red Star away by the half hour mark. A goal within ninety seconds from Viollet after being set up by Taylor gave an instant cushion on the first leg one goal lead then Bobby Charlton scored two different type of goals, one a net buster the other completing a fine team move. 3-0 on the day, 5-1 on aggregate made for a good half time drink.

Like Arsenal though, Red Star came out a different side and scored quickly in the second half and then got a disputed penalty as Tasic fell over Bill Foulkes, then got up and scored from the spot. This lifted the Belgrade crowd but United seemed to be holding onto what was now a two goal advantage when Harry Gregg slithered out of his area, carrying the ball. The resultant free kick took a deflection past Gregg and with three minutes left it was really game on. Luckily United held onto their one goal advantage and gratefully got back into their dressing room in the semi final of the European Cup for the second successive season. There, Bert Whalley and Tom Curry had sorted bottles of beer for the lads to celebrate with and an impromptu party was on the go. This continued later at a party arranged by the British Embassy in Belgrade, before pockets of the players slipped off either back to the hotel or into the city for some more celebration.

Thursday 6th February 1958
Some people were nursing hang over's as the party of players, journalists and officials made its way to Zenum airport for the return journey to Manchester, again via Munich. The journey across East Europe to Germany was a decent one, but they were greeted with thick snow as they landed in Munich. The first take off to Manchester was aborted when the two pilots detected an uneven engine sound. The attempt at take off was made again but forty seconds later the same thing happened and the plane came to an halt halfway down the runway. This time the pilots decided on disembarking to ascertain the problems.

Many thought that this would mean an overnight stay in Munich, but much to the surprise of most, the pilot informed that they were happy to fly on. There was no definite seating plan so the party sat where they wanted as the plane taxied and was ready for take off. The plane made its way along the runway amidst a howling and whistling sound when BANG! Passengers and luggage were scattered all over the place, there was an explosion and the back end of the plane broke off and burst into flames. The rest is history...

The team that was the 'Busby Babes' was no more. Captain Roger Byrne, his understudy Geoff Bent, little Eddie Colman who I had seen play his debut only two and a bit years ago at Bolton, Mark Jones the genial giant of a centre half, Liam (Billy) Whelan the graceful goal scoring inside right, Tommy Taylor the greatest centre forward in the world and the flying winger David Pegg were all killed outright. The might of British journalism was also wiped out. Alf Clarke who bled the Manchester United red in his writing, Tom Jackson a fellow Manchester journalist of Clarke and like him a contributor to the club programme 'United Review', Frank Swift formally one of England's greatest ever goalkeepers now a News of The World journalist, Don Davies known as 'Old International', Eric Thornton of The Mail, Henry Rose of The Express, Archie Ledbrooke of The Mirror and George Follows of The Herald. Three of Manchester United's vital backroom staff in Walter Crickmer club Secretary, Tom Curry the trainer and Bert Whalley the assistant coach also perished. Three others on board, Walter Satinoff, B.P.Miklos and W.T.Cable were amongst the twenty one people to be killed outright.

Fifteen days after the crash, the lad who had become a man, already amongst the greatest players in the world, and to this day counted as Manchester United's finest footballer, Duncan Edwards died of his injuries. Let the words of Robert Browning be his epitaph;

> *'One who never turned his back but marched breast forward.*
> *Never doubted clouds would break,*
> *Never dreamed, though right was worsted, wrong would triumph,*
> *Held we fall to rise, are baffled to fight better,*
> *Sleep to wake'*

In later life I had the real honour and pleasure of writing biographies on Duncan Edwards(with Iain McCartney) and Eddie Colman and Geoff Bent in 'A Salford Lad', along with meeting some of the survivors, writing 'Viollet' (with Brian Hughes MBE) and hosting sports dinners with Jackie Blanchflower. I also had the real pleasure and distinct honour of having the only Journalist survivor, Frank Taylor, give a vote of thanks to a speech I did in deepest Barnsley, birthplace of Mark Jones and Tommy Taylor.

After a week of the heaviest snowfall Old Trafford took on an Alpine look for the 4th Round Cup Tie versus Ipswich. Here a shot from Viollet (extreme right) tests Ipswich goalkeeper Bailey whilst Malcolm runs in from the left. Scanlon is poised to the rear. The shot missed but two others didn't making the score 2-0. *Photo by courtesy of the Daily Mail*

As I said earlier, in my opinion the term the 'Busby Babes' was meant for a group of footballers who progressed Matt Busby's vision following his league title success in 1952, through to having a regular supply of young players to fit in with his footballing philosophy. That produced further titles in 1956 and 1957 and was on the cusp of a double only to lose the 1957 FA Cup Final in controversial circumstances, along with threatening to conquer Europe on the footballing fields of that continent. To complete the diary of 1957/58, the first team finished in ninth place, the reserves in third place. We lost the FA Cup Final to Bolton 2-0, and lost in the semi finals of the European Cup 5-2 on aggregate to AC Milan. The FA Youth Cup team lost in the semi final to Wolves, although two of the team, Alex Dawson and Mark Pearson had to play for the first team the night before one of the legs due to the player shortage.

That team the 'Busby Babes' died in Munich in February 1958...

Chapter THIRTEEN
So, Just who were The Busby Babes?

The term 'Busby Babes' evolved around the time Matt Busby quickened the process of bringing his youthful players through in 1953. Jimmy Murphy and Matt identified the urgent need to replace the brilliant 1948 FA Cup winners and 1952 League Champions, whose age, and not least time spent away in the Second World War ,threatened to leave Manchester United adrift.

In 1953 the creation of the FA Youth Cup was a great boost to see how far, and how quick, his batch of young players, recruited from all over Britain, would be able to see Manchester United as the top side again. It was credited to Tom Jackson of the Manchester Evening News to call the side the 'Busby Babes' after a friendly at Kilmarnock which preceded some of them playing in the first team fixture against Huddersfield Town. At that time 'Babes' they may have been but they were soon men, as Manchester United won two successive championships and were the talk of all Europe as the team beat all but the truly great Real Madrid.

As a boy of that era, I always associated a certain eleven as the 'Busby Babes' beat all before them; WOOD, FOULKES, BYRNE (Capt) COLMAN, JONES, EDWARDS, BERRY, WHELAN, TAYLOR, VIOLLET and PEGG. These players rarely were rested, but injuries and of course the playing of Internationals on days when league fixtures took place, meant that others had to be involved. If you take 1954/55 as the beginning of Manchester United's new look side till that fateful day in Munich in February 1958 when they were decimated, the following also had more than bit parts to help the team succeed as they did; GREGG, GREAVES, BENT, WHITEFOOT, GOODWIN, BLANCHFLOWER, McGUINNESS, MORGANS, CHARLTON,DOHERTY, WEBSTER, and SCANLON.

Let us now have a look individually at these men who were tagged the 'BUSBY BABES' RAY WOOD: Goalkeeper, tall and lean. As a boy he was my hero. I always liked that green jersey he wore, another splash of colour alongside his red shirted team mates at a time when life was really colourless, grey, and drab in the early 1950's. Ray was one of the few players Matt Busby paid a transfer fee for in the period 1945-1958. He was bought from Darlington and played three times for England. A steady, reliable keeper with no frills, Ray was a great professional with a laid back attitude. He gave Manchester United great service until being replaced by Harry Gregg a couple of months before Munich. Survived the crash and went onto play elsewhere and then coach all around the world. BILL FOULKES: Right Full Back. Affectionately known as 'Cowboy' because of his bandy legs, Bill eventually played over 650 matches for Manchester United, receiving just one England cap. A teak-tough, straight faced and uncomplicated player, after surviving the crash he later switched to centre half and won two more Championship medals, an FA Cup medal, and fittingly, a European Cup medal in 1968, having scored a rare, vital goal against Real Madrid along the way.

ROGER BYRNE: Captain and Left Full Back. A class player, Roger played 33 consecutive games for England up to Munich and must surely rate amongst the best left backs ever to play for England. I believe he would have been the man to captain England after the forthcoming 1958 World Cup Finals in Sweden but for the disaster. With the speed as a former left winger, he was tough and could be cantankerous at times. He had played in 1952 championship side. Roger was an intelligent person who was studying to become a physiotherapist in preparation for when his playing days were over. Well respected by players and management, Roger was a captain who led by example.

EDDIE COLMAN; Right Half. A Salford lad through and through, Eddie was the cheeky chappie of the team, always ready for a laugh and a joke, he loved playing pranks on his team mates and training staff at Old Trafford. Eddie was also known as the player with the Marilyn Monroe wiggle when he played and was potentially one of the greatest right half's in Britain. Immensely liked by all his team mates, his death cost not only Manchester United, but England a true star.

MARK JONES; Centre Half. Mark was a giant of a man, standing six foot one inch and tipping the scales at fourteen stones. He was one of three Yorkshire lads in the team. He and Jackie Blanchflower were in constant competition for the centre half spot. Mark was a big powerful stopper who feared nothing or nobody on the field. Off the field he was a quiet pipe smoker and budgie breeder. He was unlucky that Billy Wright was captain of England and regarded as an institution, which prevented Mark from being a regular International.

DUNCAN EDWARDS: Left Half. Nearly said could write a book about Duncan, I have already had that honour! Did the original biography in conjunction with Iain McCartney and you felt as though you could just write and write about him, and he was only twenty one when his injuries took him away from us. Many have had the tag the 'next' Duncan Edwards but none have lasted the test of time. Indeed, I feel the only one you could compare was also of his generation, John Charles. Duncan could literally play in any position. I saw him play at number five, six, nine and ten. Pass, shoot, tackle, head, run, Duncan was top class in all he did. He already had eighteen England caps at twenty one and surely would have been an eventual England captain. It is not fanciful to feel he and not Bobby Moore, would have been lifting that World Cup in 1966 as Duncan would have only been twenty nine on that day. The official Manchester United ledger showed he was the highest paid player at the time of his death on £37 a week.

JOHNNY BERRY; Outside Right. From the young Duncan to the oldest player of this side and also the smallest. Whilst he might have been small in stature, he had a massive heart and tons of ability. One of the very few who cost a fee, signing from Birmingham City in 1951. A dribbling winger he could beat men inside or on the outside. Played for England four times, but it took the likes of Stanley Matthews and Tom Finney to mean he did not play more. Suffered terrible injuries in the crash, never played again.

LIAM (BILLY) WHELAN; Inside Right. A quite superb footballer, who probably did not believe himself just how good he was. Whilst looked languid, he had marvellous control and a real goal scorer's touch. Lost his place a couple of months before the crash to Bobby Charlton and it is by no means certain that he would not have got it back. Capped by his native Eire four times he was a staunch catholic whose religion gave him great strength at Munich.

TOMMY TAYLOR; Centre Forward. The costliest player of the Busby Babes following his transfer from Barnsley in 1953 for £29,999. Known as the 'Smiling Executioner' he was quite simply the finest centre forward in Manchester United's history. Tall, a great header of the ball but very good on the ground, his goal scoring record also stands the test of time in the record books. England's centre forward at the time of his death, he was a certainty for the forthcoming World Cup finals in Sweden.

DENNIS VIOLLET; Inside Left. A great footballer. Another player I had the honour of writing a biography, this one with Brian Hughes MBE. A Manchester lad through and through ,he was a very clever player who scored more than a fair share of goals. Scored Manchester United's first ever European goal and still holds the record number of league goals in a season for the club. Was very surprising the lack of England caps he received, he actually played twice. Survived the crash, but was a strange transfer away to Stoke City in 1962. There, he combined with Stanley Matthew to bring the club back to former glories before moving to set up life in America. A top bloke.

DAVID PEGG; Outside Left. A good looking lad, he was a fine left winger who had one England cap at the time of the crash. Vied with Albert Scanlon for this number eleven spot, but Pegg was a top class player. If he had survived, he would have, with his good looks, been a real star when footballers became like pop stars in the 1960's.

So, that was the acknowledged first eleven but as I mention earlier there was another side that could have got those places on another day. Let's have a look at them now;

JACKIE BLANCHFLOWER; Centre Half or Inside Forward. Was starting to make his mark as inside right, but the competition from John Doherty and then Billy Whelan meant his versatility came in really handy. Moved to centre half, and in a lot of ways played his finest football. It was really a case of who was in the position between him and Mark Jones as to who got a run in the side. Neither wanted to be hurt because they knew a spell out could be for a while. His brother, Danny, was a top class player for Tottenham Hotspur, the pair of them bedrocks of the Northern Ireland side. Like Johnny Berry, suffered terrible injuries in the crash and never played again. He became a very good after dinner speaker once telling me a lovely story about Johnny Berry. Jackie remembered a game early in his career at Bolton Wanderers. "Bolton away was always a difficult match for us. One game Johnny Berry said to me, 'when you see Duncan get the ball let us do a scissors movement and you come out to the wing'. Now this surprised me as Johnny always hugged the line. Anyhow, when Duncan got the ball me and Johnny switched, next thing I am waking up in Bolton Infirmary as their left back Tommy Banks had sent me flying over the paddock wall!"

IAN GREAVES; Full Back. It always seems that Billy Foulkes was first choice right back, but Ian got into the side in the 1955/56 season, held his place, and won a championship medal. Did not go to Munich and after the crash became a first choice. Injury cost him dear, but in later life became a fine manager, particularly at Huddersfield Town and Bolton Wanderers. Indeed, there was a school of thought that he might have become a Manchester United manager.

JEFF WHITEFOOT; Right Half. Still the youngest player to start a match for Manchester United at 16 years and 105 days. A very fine right half it seemed he would fill a tricky position for Manchester United but the rise of the brilliant Eddie Colman cost him a place in the eventual great side the 'Busby Babes' Went onto play excellently for Nottingham Forest.

JOHN DOHERTY; Inside Right. Fate played a big part in John's career. Having established himself as the youth team inside right, injury cost him a place in the first final of that competition and the club went and brought Billy Whelan over for the game. John Doherty then re established himself as the first team inside right before Whelan's exceptional skill earned him the first team number eight shirt. Bobby Charlton of course, came along later but by then John Doherty had moved onto play for Leicester City.

COLIN WEBSTER; Versatile Forward. Colin earns that title of versatile as he played at numbers seven, eight, nine, ten and eleven for the club. Colin Joined after a recommendation from Dennis Viollet when they did National Service. Scored many vital goals for the 'Busby Babes' but never really earned a first choice on merit. Caught flu on the weekend before Munich so missed the fateful flight. Played four times for his native Wales, appearing for them in the World Cup quarter finals against Brazil in 1958.

FREDDIE GOODWIN; Right Half. Whilst never in the same level as Eddie Colman, Freddie was an excellent replacement when required. Tall, he did not travel to Munich, he was an automatic inclusion afterwards. The signing of Maurice Setters cost him his place and he moved to Leeds United where he had a decent career. Also a fine cricketer, he played county cricket for Lancashire as a fast bowler.

GEOFF BENT; Left Back. A really tragic combination of events cost Geoff his life, and a first class career. He played in the reserves on the Saturday before the crash and was not down for travelling. An injury worry over captain Roger Byrne meant it was Geoff and not Ronnie Cope who travelled. In the event, Roger played and both of them perished. The extra tragedy was that he would have been the natural replacement after for Roger and Geoff was such a good left back who knows how far his career might have gone?

WILF McGUINNESS; Left Half. A bubbly, capable footballer, Wilf had the unenviable position of being Duncan Edwards replacement. Wilf did not travel to Munich due to a previous injury and was given the number six shirt when he was fit. He later went onto play for England before a broken leg virtually ended his career. Turning to coaching, Wilf was an assistant to Alf Ramsey in the successful 1966 World Cup Finals for England. He then was made Manchester United coach after Matt Busby's retirement.

ALBERT SCANLON; Outside Left. The word character summed up Albert. Nicknames abound about him, Joe Friday, Albert the Docker are just two! An excellent left winger who delivered a great cross, Albert vied with David Pegg for the number eleven shirt, having won his big chance on merit a couple of months before Munich. He survived the crash and came back to have two brilliant seasons. Like the transfer of Dennis Viollet, Albert left Manchester United suddenly, probably his off field escapades catching up with him.

HARRY GREGG; Goalkeeper. A quite brilliant goalkeeper, a very charismatic man, and ultimately a Manchester United hero. Harry signed a couple of months before Munich in a record transfer after a superb display for his native Northern Ireland at Wembley. He always oozed class and confidence, his actions in the crash made him a hero due to his sheer bravery. He survived the crash and was Manchester United's number one for a number of years, injury also seeming to deprive him of a medal when one was on offer.

KENNY MORGANS; Outside Right. That he had replaced the mature, excellent Johnny Berry a couple of months before the crash at the young age of eighteen, showed how much Matt Busby regarded this player. He was a direct winger who survived the crash. Never able to regain the form that he was capable of sadly.

This leaves just one further Manchester United player who graced the side titled the 'Busby Babes'.

BOBBY CHARLTON; Inside Forward, Centre Forward, Left Wing. Bobby became the golden boy for both Manchester United and England. He had played games mainly as a replacement for Whelan, Taylor or Viollet, before winning a first team place on merit a couple of months before the crash. After the crash all the hopes of Manchester United's future seemed to be on his shoulders, but he handled the expectation brilliantly. Playing in different positions, including a long spell for club and country on the left wing, he went onto captain Manchester United to the European Cup in 1968, having been a vital member of England's World Cup winning side two years earlier. The words legend, great, just sit comfortably on his shoulders.

So, there we have twenty three players who made a huge contribution to a side tagged the 'Busby Babes' A side that lifted everybody who saw them around Britain and Europe. A side which was about to confirm its maturity as one of the game's greatest sides. A side which was wiped out in an unimaginable tragedy at the end of a German runway.

Chapter FOURTEEN
What If?

The side that last represented Manchester United in Belgrade on 5th February 1958 contained many young players. This has always opened the door to what if they had lived? How far would they have gone, and would those that followed have been signed, or fitted in with the side that last, fateful day?

Those that played on 5th Feb 1958 were; GREGG, FOULKES, BYRNE, COLMAN, JONES, EDWARDS, MORGANS, CHARLTON, TAYLOR, VIOLLET and SCANLON. Certainly, BENT, BLANCHFLOWER, McGUINNESS, WHELAN, and PEGG were definitely still in the frame to contribute with this side, whilst DAWSON and PEARSON were also very close to be really challenging. Lower down the junior ranks at the time of the crash were GASKELL, STILES, GILES and BRENNAN.

If you went forward five years, Manchester United next won a trophy when they lifted the FA Cup by beating Leicester City 3-1 at Wembley Stadium, the side that day was; GASKELL, DUNNE, CANTWELL, CRERAND, FOULKES, SETTERS, GILES, QUIXALL, HERD, LAW and CHARLTON. As you can see, Billy Foulkes and Bobby Charlton played in both matches, although in different positions. Harry Gregg was still on the playing books but, sadly, had started to suffer injuries, particularly shoulder ones, which cost him a medal in 1963 and a league title in 1965.This is where David Gaskell came in. John Giles progressed to the first team, whilst Shay Brennan and Nobby Stiles, Stiles in particular, was around the squad of 1963.Wilf McGuinness was on the coaching staff in 1963, although still a young man, a broken leg virtually ended his career in 1959 but he made a very successful career as a coach. Of the others from 1958 who had lived, Kenny Morgans, Dennis Viollet and Albert Scanlon had moved on from Old Trafford by 1963, whilst Jackie Blanchflower and Johnny Berry were never fit to play again.

Those different from 1963 to 1958 are in the interesting category. Tony Dunne became a brilliant full back, able to play either right or left back. He joined Manchester United as a young man from Southern Ireland and it is more than conceivable that he would still have done so. By 1963 Roger Byrne would have been thirty four and Dunne would have made a perfect replacement. In saying that, so would Geoff Bent if he had been spared. This opens the question of would Noel Cantwell have been signed by United? He was a fine player and leader and Matt Busby may have decided he was a quality replacement for Roger by 1960. Pat Crerand is one of the most intriguing players when you wonder what if. In 1963, Eddie Colman would still have only been twenty six, probably an England regular, would Pat have been a requirement? One signature Matt Busby would not have had to make was Maurice Setters as Duncan Edwards would have only been, like Eddie Colman, twenty six. Along, of course, with being the World's greatest footballer. This leaves the inside forward trio of 1963, and interesting possibilities...

I suspect Albert Quixall would not have been a signature, certainly not at a record £45,000, that Matt Busby would have made. By 1963 Bobby Charlton was only twenty five, whilst Billy Whelan if had been spared would have only been twenty seven. David Herd could easily have been on the radar though, Tommy Taylor would have been thirty one by 1963 and Herd was a big favourite of Matt Busby from a long way back. The big doubt would have been the progress of Alex Dawson. He would have been twenty three in 1963, eventually moving to Preston North End. What affect did the crash have on his progress though? He was scoring goals for fun in 1958 when only eighteen and looked Taylor's natural replacement. Then there is the man who became King of Old Trafford, Denis Law. A true World class player, a man Matt Busby had coveted since he was at Huddersfield Town in their youth side, and later managed at Scotland level. I am convinced he would have still joined United, particularly as there was obviously something in the air between the also great Dennis Viollet and Matt Busby. Putting Bobby Charlton back as number eight would have been easier as David Pegg would still only have been twenty seven in 1963. Wembley Stadium, therefore, could have seen this Manchester United side taking the field of play; GASKELL (or a fit GREGG), DUNNE, CANTWELL, COLMAN, FOULKES, EDWARDS, GILES, CHARLTON, HERD, LAW and PEGG.

This is how Manchester United could have evolved by 1963, five years after that in 1968; Manchester United finally lifted their Holy Grail, the European Cup. This was ten years after the Munich air disaster, what would the sides of 1958 and 1963 look like by 1968? The Manchester United side that beat Benfica 4-1 in late May 1968, also at Wembley Stadium, was; STEPNEY, BRENNAN, DUNNE, CRERAND, FOULKES, STILES, BEST, KIDD, CHARLTON, SADLER and ASTON. By then, Harry Gregg had left United and a top class goalkeeper was a necessity. Alex Stepney filled that bill. Shay Brennan had persevered with his Manchester United career from the junior sides of 1958 and was comfortable at right back. Tony Dunne had become that outstanding left back and was a regular. The right half position is still a huge question mark. Eddie Colman would have been thirty one by 1968, although Pat Crerand was twenty nine himself. Would he have ever been a Manchester United player? It has to be said that Matt Busby always rated Pat very highly, so I suspect it would have depended on how Eddie Colman's career had panned out. Billy Foulkes was now the rock of the Manchester United defence, as with Bobby Charlton the only survivors from ten years back at first team level. The number six shirt is a highly emotive one...

Duncan Edwards would have been, like Colman, thirty one. It is not fanciful to consider that he would have been Manchester United captain, probably England's as well. Indeed, it surely would have been him, not Bobby Moore, who had lifted the World Cup in 1966. Nobby Stiles himself became a true Manchester United favourite. He had the ability to play in various roles, playing at numbers two, four, six and eight for the club. Perhaps he would have been thrown into the pot for the number four shirt with Eddie Colman and Pat Crerand?

The 1968 forward line that represented Manchester United all came through their youth system. George Best had joined in 1962 from school, Brian Kidd was just eighteen in May 1968, Bobby Charlton had been an original Busby Babe, David Sadler came from school in 1962 like Best, and John Aston, son of one of the original Manchester United greats from 1948, was in his early twenties in 1968. The only difference would have been the inclusion of Denis Law, who was unfit for the 1968 final. That team, therefore, that finally lifted the trophy which so many had given so much for on behalf of Manchester United could have been; STEPNEY, BRENNAN, DUNNE, COLMAN (or CRERAND or STILES) FOULKES, EDWARDS, BEST, LAW, CHARLTON, SADLER and ASTON. Just look at those numbers six, seven, eight and nine!

The commentary could have gone, "The ball is picked up by Edwards, a glorious sweeping pass to the right wing to Best. He collects, drops a shoulder, flights the ball over to the edge of the penalty area for Charlton to meet on the volley. What a shot, what a save but the keeper spills it and there is Law to turn into the net".

A glorious dream of an unfulfilled one...

15846396R00051

Printed in Great Britain
by Amazon